BY JOHN MCPHEE

La Place de la Concorde Suisse

JOHN McPHEE

La Place de la Concorde Suisse

The Noonday Press

Farrar, Straus and Giroux

NEW YORK

Copyright © 1983, 1984 by John McPhee
All rights reserved
Printed in the United States of America
Published in Canada by Macfarlane Walter & Ross
First published in 1984 by Farrar, Straus and Giroux
First published by The Noonday Press in 1991
Thirteenth printing, 1996
Library of Congress Cataloging-in-Publication Data
McPhee, John A.
La place de la concorde suisse.
UA800.M3   1984   355'.0330494   83-27466
The text of this book originally appeared in
The New Yorker and was developed with the editorial
counsel of William Shawn and C. P. Crow

For my daughters in their Wanderjahre

La Place de la Concorde Suisse

The Swiss have not fought a war for nearly five hundred years, and are determined to know how so as not to.

In Italy, it has been said of the Swiss Army, "I didn't know they had one." When the Italian learns that the Swiss Army vastly outnumbers Italy's, the Italian says, "That is not difficult."

The Swiss Army has served as a model for less languid nations. The Israeli Army is a copy of the Swiss Army.

Switzerland is two times the size of New Jersey. New Jersey, by far, has the larger population. Nonetheless, there are six hundred and fifty thousand people in the Swiss Army. At any given time, most of them are walking around in street clothes or in blue from the collar down. They are a civilian army, a trained and practiced militia, ever ready to mobilize. They serve for thirty years. All six hundred and fifty thousand are prepared to be present at mobilization points and battle stations in considerably less than forty-eight hours.

If you understand the New York Yacht Club, the Cosmos Club, the Metropolitan Club, the Century Club, the Piedmont Driving Club, you would understand the Swiss Army.

Some of these thoughts run through my mind as the Section de Renseignements—of the Eighth Battalion of the Fifth Regiment of the Tenth Mountain Division —gets ready to patrol a sector of the uppermost Rhone. The battalion has been told to move, and it is the business of these soldiers to learn as thoroughly and as rapidly as they can what their major needs to know about the new sector; for example, how many troops will fit in a cable car to the Riederalp? Where is a good site for a command post on the lower declivities of the alp above Lax? How many soldiers could sleep in the Schwarzenbach barn? Would that be all right with Schwarzenbach? Have explosives already been installed—as is the case at thousands of strategic points in Switzerland—to blow up the Nussbaum bridge?

With notebooks and pencils, the patrols of the Section de Renseignements go from place to place exploring, asking questions, collecting particulars, scribbling information, characterizing and describing people and scenes, doing reconnaissance of various terrains, doing surveillance of present activity, and tracking events of the recent past. Afterward, they trudge back and, under pressure of time, compress, arrange, and present what they have heard and seen. All of that is incorporated into the substance of the word "renseignements."

I have limitless empathy for the Section de Renseignements. The leader of the second patrol today is Luc Massy, who entered the army ten years ago with essentially his present status. He is five feet eleven inches tall, with blond hair and an aquiline nose—trim, irreverent, thirty years old. The others are Jean-Bruno Wettstein, Denis Schyrr, Pierre Pera, Jean Reidenbach. Each wears boots, gaiters, a mountain jacket, and a woolly-earflap Finnish hat, and carries a fusil d'assaut, which can fire twenty-four bullets in eight seconds and, with added onomatopoeia, is also know as a Sturmgewehr. Massy wears hobnailed boots. Most of the other soldiers are younger, and when they came into the army were issued boots with rubber soles—Swiss crosses protruding from the soles in lieu of hobnails. Massy says he feels the north wind, and therefore the weather will be stable for three, six, or nine days. The air seems still to me—a clear and frosted morning at the end of October in a deep valley under Alps freshly dusted with snow. Using pocket calculators and topographic maps, the patrol has charted its assignments—uphill, down, up, down—figuring that eleven hours will be required to complete them. Accordingly, each man puts in his pack a plastic sack of lunch and a plastic sack of dinner—dried fruit, fresh fruit, bread, cheese, pâté, sausage, and bars that are labelled "Militärschokolade, Chocolat Militaire."

This is the Valais, the Swiss canton with the country's highest mountains—a canton divided by the west-running Rhone, which once flowed as ice five thousand feet deep to cut among the mountains its otherwise irrational groove. The Alps crowd the great chasm—off the left bank the Pennines, off the right bank the Bernese Oberland. The canton is divided in language as well, part French, part German, and not in a mixed-up manner, which would be utterly un-Swiss, but with a break that is clear in the march of towns—Champéry, Martigny, Sion, Sierre, Salgesch, Turtmann, Ausserberg, Brig—and clearer still in the names of the hanging valleys that come down among the peaks and plummet to the Rhone: Val de Bagnes, Val d'Hérens, Val d'Anniviers, Turtmanntal, Lötschental, Mattertal. The Tenth Mountain Division consists almost wholly of Suisses romands, as French-speaking Swiss are known. In their present exercises, they are well spread out through French and German Valais. In the German-speaking villages, soldiers puzzle at the names of streets and shops and understand nothing of the talk they overhear.

The divisionnaire of the Tenth Mountain Division is, of course, from French Switzerland—La Suisse Romande, also known as La Romandie. His name is Adrien Tschumy. On his shoulders—and nested in the fleece of his Finnish hat—are pairs of stars. There is a Swiss cross in the center of each star. The Divisionnaire is tall, trim, contemplative, with dark hair, a narrow face, and a manner that is quietly convincing. In military roles, the film actor Gregory Peck has resembled Tschumy, who resembles General MacArthur.

Tschumy must go to remote places to see his men in action. In Switzerland, there are no Fort Hoods, Fort Irwins, no vast terrains set aside for explosive games. There are few barracks. Troops on active duty for refresher courses (also known as repetition courses) are quartered for the most part in villages and towns, and if they are using live ammunition they must walk to far places to shoot. Here, for instance, Tschumy visits a company of grenadiers in the morning shadow of the Torrenthorn, six thousand feet above the Rhone. The Swiss Army grenadiers look upon themselves in the way that the United States Marines look upon themselves. The Swiss Army grenadiers specialize in events that take place at two thousand metres and skyward. They are technical climbers, schussbooming skiers, demolition experts, and crack shots, who sleep on granite mattresses and eat chocolate-coated nails. Some of them are bankers. Others are chauffeurs, dental technicians, civil engineers, alpine guides. They have discovered an enemy command post and are moving in its direction under the covering fire of automatic rifles. The bullets are bullets. Signal flags, understood all over Switzerland, have been set out to advertise the danger to passing promeneurs. Moving uphill, up a small cirque valley, the soldiers advance behind exploding grenades. Officers observe. One lieutenant works for I.B.M. in White Plains, New York, and has taken three weeks off to do his service. Crawling through snow under more bullets, the grenadiers reach the wall of the command post, a dotted line in their minds, and lay beside it a high-explosive plastic. They run. Chunks of broken rock rise out of the snow and fly in all directions, as much as three hundred metres—some above the head of the Divisionnaire. Like a theatre, the reverberant cirque enhances the explosion.

Meanwhile, certain boulders across a ravine have been identified as enemy helicopters that have just landed. For seven hundred years, Swiss soldiers have been masters of the mountain pass, and have looked upon the high divides not only as standpoints of invincible defense but as virtual weapons in themselves—terrain where the alien was disadvantaged and the Swiss could win battles even with falling rocks. Helicopters flout the mountain pass. The flying horses, as they are regarded, can appear from anywhere, come whirling over some unlikely arête, and with machine guns firing drop soldiers in the snow. The defense adapts. Men with bazookas on their backs run toward the helicopters and fall prone while their partners aim the tubes and fire. Explosions turn the choppers into scree.

Now the grenadiers discover the existence of an

enemy radio shack farther up the valley. They go after it with a blend of automatic rifles and grenades, crawling under the rifle fire to heave the grenades. The noise is loud to the point of pain, and the observing officers have fingers in their ears. Bullets rain on the mountain wall. The soldiers run forward, hide behind rocks. Grenades explode. As the soldiers move up the valley—now running low, now crawling, now inching along on their chests—a corporal walks upright behind them, like a football coach following the progress of a scrimmage. Wooden silhouettes representing enemy soldiers are blown and shot to bits. The objective is reached, and, with a final rush—with an explosion louder than any that has come before—the radio shack is taken without prisoners.

Walking back to lower ground, the Divisionnaire has many points to teach. Characteristically, he taps one index finger on the other as he talks. His primary point seems to be that the officers' preparation should have been more thorough. Intent on what he is saying, he does not look up. If he did, he could see out of Switzerland. He could see Mont Blanc, twice his altitude, bright in the morning light, and in Swiss terrain the Grand Combin, the Dent Blanche, the Weisshorn—a freshened sea of peaks beyond the deep airspace of the invisible Rhone. Resting level on rock and snow, a table has been set, with a red tablecloth; and the sun—at half past nine—has come over the Torrenthorn to shine on silver platters of rolled shaved beef, bacon, sausages, wedges of tomato, half-sliced pickles in the shape of fans. Officers stand around the table. There is a company of teacups in close ranks, another of stemmed glassware. There are baskets of bread. The wines are of the Valais. The red is Chapelle de Salquenen. The rosé is Œil de Perdrix, in a bucket full of snow. Tschumy drinks a cup of tea. A promeneur happens by—a citizen in knickers, boots, heavy socks, a mountain hat—on his way from who knows to where. He just appears, like a genie. His appearance suggests that he is above fifty and done with the army. He absorbs the scene: the festive table, the officers sipping and nibbling and quietly debriefing, the soldiers at a distance sitting in clusters on their packs, the charcoal streaks on the exploded snow. "Gut," he says, and he waves and walks on.

"Wiedersehen," the Divisionnaire calls after him, and the Divisionnaire is himself soon away—rising into the air in his Alouette III, his French six-seat jet-powered chopper, ascending among walls of red rock to cross into the Lötschental. Trending northeast, the valley rises toward the center of the Bernese Oberland. It is possible in Switzerland to be so far above and away from the Mittelland—the smooth perfected country that runs from Lake Geneva through Bern and Zurich—that even a Swiss valley, like the rough young mountains surrounding it, may seem penarctic and remote. The Lötschental is such a valley. The people of the Lötschental live in small, dark-cabin towns. A stream flows among them, pushing boulders. High serrated mountains are lined up in rows on either side, and the valley floor rises between them into fields of perennial snow. There are charcoal streaks on the snow. In the last five miles of the Lötschental, moving glacier ice is packed between the summits and leads to a gap where the converging mountains all but close. Twenty-five, twenty-six, twenty-seven hundred metres, the ice bends upward like the tip of a ski. Passing three thousand metres, the helicopter floats up a face of rock and moves through the gap into a world too bright for unshielded eyes. It is the top of the Bernese Oberland, where ice fields and snowfields are the white diameters of circumvallate arêtes, where all horizons are violent. The granite Jungfrau, the Mönch, the Eiger, the Fiescherhorn, the Aletschhorn, the Fiescher Gabelhorn conduct the eye across the glaciers to the gneisses of the Aar massif, to the obeliscal Finsteraarhorn, four thousand two hundred and seventy-three metres, the highest mountain north of the Rhone. Crystallizing and recrystallizing, the ice among the peaks collects and compacts itself into the Grosser Aletschgletscher, the supreme glacier of Europe, with avenues of ice coming in from six or eight directions to conjoin in a frozen intersection officially identified on maps as Konkordiaplatz, La Place de la Concorde Suisse. The Divisionnaire looks about him with a thoughtful smile. This place that will never need defending represents what the Swiss defend. In surroundings quieter than a jet-driven helicopter, I have heard him say that he is without reservation "persuadé de la valeur de l'effort de défense"—so thoroughly persuaded, in fact, that he gave up a career as a hydroelectric engineer to devote full time to the army. When he was a part-time artillery officer, rising to colonel, he was a civilian concerned primarily with the efficiency of turbines, which he understood so well that he practiced his trade not only in all parts of Switzerland but also from China to Chile to Hydro-Quebec. A couple of years ago, when he was fifty, he was invited to become an army professional.

The professionals are less than half of one per cent of the Swiss Army. They are not only officers but people of almost all ranks and specialties, who teach the militia the ways of war and help make the militia cohesive. Tschumy was given two stars for his hat and his epaulets, and responsibility for the Tenth Mountain Division. One star signifies a brigadier, and three stars a commandant de corps. There are seven commandants de corps, the highest-ranking officers in the army. The word "general" is not used except in situations of extreme emergency, when a fourth star is presented to one leader, chosen by the Federal Assembly.

In five centuries of neutrality, Switzerland has had four generals. The first was Guillaume-Henri Dufour, who was appointed in 1847 to suppress a rebellion of seven Catholic cantons: Lucerne, Uri, Schwyz, Unterwalden, Zug, Fribourg, and Valais. Neutrality does not exclude civil war. Dufour pounded the Catholics, who gave up after twenty-seven days. With paradoxical obscurity, his name rests on Dufourspitze, one of the least-known summits in the world, although it is the highest in Switzerland. Never mind that like the Matterhorn it is half Italian. Switzerland's other generals were appointed at times of nervous mobilization at the borders, of fearing what might happen as a result of proximate wars. General Hans Herzog became a national hero as the principal spectator of the Franco-Prussian War. In the First World War, General Ulrich Wille led the Swiss to victory. Victory consisted of successfully avoiding the conflict. As someone put it, "we won by having no war." In the Second World War, the victorious Swiss general was Henri Guisan, of the Canton de Vaud. There

La Place de la Concorde Suisse

is a General Guisan Quai in Zurich, a Quai Général Guisan in Geneva. In every part of Switzerland, there are streets and plazas and equestrian statues—there are busts on plinths overhung with banners and flags—doing honor to the general of an army that did not fight. Switzerland defends itself on what it calls the Porcupine Principle. You roll up into a ball and brandish your quills. In the words of Divisionnaire Tschumy, "The foremost battle is to prevent war with a price of entry that is too high. You must understand that there is no difference between the Swiss people and the Swiss Army. There is no difference in will. Economic, military—it's the same thing. For seven hundred years, freedom has been the fundamental story of Switzerland, and we are not prepared to give it up now. We want to defend ourselves, which is not the same as fighting abroad. We want peace, but not under someone else's conditions. We will fight from the border. In response to a ground attack, which would in all likelihood come from the northeast, we intend to keep a maximum proportion of our land free. There are those who think we should train only for guerrilla warfare. That would be a form of giving up. Another possibility is that someone might use Switzerland by going through a corner or two, or to get to the north by the Simplon Pass or the pass of Grand-Saint-Bernard. We must stop that, too. We can really do something. We haven't enough tanks, but, given the nature of our terrain, we can fight with infantry. The first days of fighting would be dangerous for us. We would lose many people. But I am confident of our defenses. If I were not confident, I would not be a divisionnaire."

Like a fly inside a chandelier, the helicopter crosses

La Place de la Concorde Suisse. Making a shortcut to
Alte Pür, it goes up the side of an arête, over the knife-
edged rock, and crosses another glacier—the Fiescher-
gletscher—under the spire of the Finsteraarhorn. It was
below the Finsteraarhorn that the Swiss first figured out
the movements and the sweeping implications of glacier
ice, dominating a world that looked something like this.
Wasenhorn, Firehorn, Chastelhorn—the mountains decline in altitude, the terrain falls toward the Rhone,
whose valley, near its beginnings, is as narrow as the
Lötschental and seems as remote. It contains two paved
airstrips—but no airport, no evident hangars, no evident
airplanes, no fuelling trucks, not even a wind sock. One
sees such airstrips in many mountain valleys. Near the
older ones are hangars that are rises in the ground. They
are painted in camouflage and covered with living grass.
Other strips are more enigmatic, since no apparent structures exist. If one just happens to be looking, though,
one might see a mountain open—might see something
like an enormous mousehole appear chimerically at the
base of an alp. Out of the mountain comes a supersonic
aircraft—a Tiger, a Mirage—bearing on its wings the
national white cross. In a matter of seconds, it is climbing
the air. Pilots sit inside the mountains waiting, night and
day. On topographic maps revised and printed since the
airstrips were built, the airstrips do not appear. The maps
are sold in bookstores all over Switzerland, but those who
wish to fill in the airstrips need their own renseignements.
Even the map on the Divisionnaire's lap does not show
the airstrips below. The Alouette crosses the Rhone, and
goes south into the small, steep-sided Blinnental. It drops
into the exact center of the V of the valley, and gradually

to the floor, not much shy of the Blinnengletscher and the international divide. The Blinnental´is essentially un-inhabited, and utterly so at Alte Pür—an alpine meadow, grazed some in summer, perhaps, but not extensively, and barren-looking now. It is a good place for artillery —a good place for forward observers to practice their art of defining the targets of the guns. Somewhere up a small valley on the north side of the Rhone is an obusier 46, which can throw fifteen kilograms ten kilometres and is practicing close to the limits of its range. The target is a cliff off the shoulder of an alp almost due south of the distant gun. Above the observers' heads, there is an occa-sional high hum, a soft whistle, as fifteen kilograms com-plete their parabola and zap the hapless alp. There is no concern whatever that if the shell should miss the alp it might go whistling into Italy. The shell is not going to miss. The observers are under camouflage nets with their field telephones and other equipment. Four such groups are in the meadow, practicing together on the same situa-tion. Their major is Jacques Hentsch, and he says the shells are taking thirty seconds to reach the target from the gun. The observers compute the difference between the intended and the actual hit. On their telephones, they present the results to the artillerymen at the gun, who make the necessary adjustments and fire again. "No prob-lem," says Major Hentsch. There is a problem, though. The calculations and the phone calls and the adjustments at the gun are supposed to take forty seconds, to which is added the thirty seconds of travel time for the ensuing shell. Now and again, a shell goes overhead and flame and thunder erupt from the alp, but not at anything approximating one-minute-and-ten-second intervals, and while the Divisionnaire—one index finger tapping against the other—speaks tensely to the observers Major Hentsch has leisure to remark that people in New York are indulging in pure hokum when they say that interest rates will continue to fall and thus the stock market is certain to go on rising. Nevertheless, he adds, New York is still one of the few places in the world where you can make money. Hentsch belongs to one of the most august and ancient private-banking families in Geneva. On his own, he has become well known for his resourceful development of new accounts. He manages portfolios. He says that he is like a priest, in that he must know his customers well in order to serve them. Less than a week ago, he was in Portland, Maine, buying lobsters. Last year, he bought twenty-five thousand lobsters, importing them through Zurich into Sweden. Of service in the Swiss Army, he says, "It belongs to the passport." And apropos of nothing at all he adds, "We are nice people. Not everyone understands that."

Why is the Divisionnaire so unhappy? With Swiss precision, every shell has exploded in an area smaller than the courtyard of the Pentagon, and the area is the target.

A communications problem, Hentsch explains, is causing the shells to come so slowly. The artillerymen at the gun are Suisses allemands, there being a shortage of artillery officers in La Suisse Romande. The forward observers are feeding back their data in French, which the people at the gun only poorly understand. The observers, for their part, observe nothing in German. The shells continue to come slowly. The shooting ends badly. A black soldier comes up to the Divisionnaire and offers him raclette for lunch. With grace, the invitation is declined.

When the Swiss Army maneuvers, the defending forces are designated blue and the enemy is red. In the Federal Assembly, the Communists complain. The Communists are one per cent, and the complaints are unavailing. This morning, as it happens, there is no enemy. The Section de Renseignements —of the Eighth Battalion of the Fifth Regiment of the Tenth Mountain Division—is collecting information from as yet uninvaded land. For Luc Massy's patrol, the starting point is the train station in Mörel, a village about seven kilometres up the Rhone from the Swiss end of the Simplon Tunnel. Sharing a bar of chocolate, the patrol is driven to Mörel in a Mercedes-Benz truck, winding through a steep country of orange tamaracks, isolated blazing maples, and the narrow cascading Rhone. "C'est loin! C'est loin!" Massy complains as each revolution of the wheels measures steps to be taken in return. Finally, as the truck noses downgrade and over railroad tracks, he says, "Voici la gare."

It is a one-metre railway, narrow-gauge and privately owned, known as the Furka-Oberalp. Four Haflingers—short and shaggy Austrian mountain horses—graze by the station. In the Swiss Army, a Haflinger is a small, tough four-wheel-drive vehicle. It is made in Austria and looks like a cross between a mule and a jeep. The téléphérique is near the station. There are two routes, and the gondolas rise more than two and a half kilometres to the shoulders of the Alps, connecting Mörel to even smaller villages above.

While passengers—apparently farmers—patiently wait, Jean-Bruno Wettstein interrogates the ticket seller. The soldiers quickly compute. An entire company could get to the top in fifty minutes.

The patrol moves out. Five hundred metres up the river is the pont de Gifrisch. The patrol stands on the bridge and carefully studies the river. Massy points.

"There is one."

"There is another."

"Three, four, five."

They are counting trout.

Their lieutenant pulls up in the Mercedes truck. Instantly, they are alert to the features of the bridge. It is a single span. It will carry twenty-eight tons. The Rhone is flowing under it at three metres per second.

Last year, the lieutenant was studying at the University of Pennsylvania. His name is Olivier Wyssa. He is from Geneva and has returned from America to practice law. He is a big man who wears light-sensitive eyeglasses and has a mustache with short handlebars.

Lieutenant Wyssa moves on. The patrol leaves the riverside and climbs the right bank a thousand vertical feet. The actual distance does not seem a great deal longer to me, as I accompany them, or, I feel sure, to them, as they labor upward with packs and rifles. The rifles weigh six and a half kilos. The packs vary. Massy says, "We are supposed to get ourselves into condition before we go to the army, but we never do."

Jean-Bruno Wettstein smiles, and remarks, "In the Suisse Romande, we say, 'Why do we go to the army, anyway? There are always enough Swiss Germans to defend us.' "

In an experience that is characteristic of the alpine-valley country, the patrol comes to a road after climbing the thousand feet. It is a shelf in the mountainside, curving into reentrants and out around promontories. A major is waiting on the road. He is driving a Pinzgauer, which is—more or less—a large Haflinger, and is also named for a horse. The major is Guy Glauser. He manufactures dental equipment in Vevey. In the army, he is in charge of all intelligence in the Fifth Regiment, and therefore of all its Sections de Renseignements. He wants to know, among other things, if the pont de Gifrisch was mined.

The answer is negative. There would not seem to be a large point in blowing up a twenty-eight-ton bridge to prevent its being crossed by a fifty-ton tank.

Returning salutes, the Major departs. The soldiers walk the road. After a bend or two, they come upon a group of workers who are patching the surface. As the patrol goes by, a man in blue overalls touches the muzzle of Denis Schyrr's gun. Schyrr says, "He inserts the flower."

We are on our way to the Nussbaum bridge, via Göuchheit, Krizacher, and Vogelture—names that to these soldiers are neither native nor foreign. The patrol drifts along, for the moment making no notes—merely covering ground, telling stories.

There is a tale about the Swiss Foreign Minister at a reception in Paris in 1979, where a kindly gentleman introduced himself as "Pierre Mendès-France."

"Pierre Aubert, Suisse," said the Foreign Minister, amiably shaking hands.

There is litter—a paper cup, a plastic bag—at the edge of the road: a remarkable sight. "Are we still in Switzerland?" asks Wettstein.

We move in and out of meadow and forest, trees at sharp angles to the ground. Where the meadows stop, the line is distinct between the varying depths of green. From the Rhodes of Appenzell to the Canton de Vaud, there is a prototypical element in the Swiss rural scene: there is no sfumato; meadows are edged absolutely by dense, dark forest. Wettstein's profession has much to do with the expectable beauty of these reiterated landscapes. He is an agronomist, thirty-two years old, and in winter he works at a Station Fédérale de Recherches Agronomiques, on an old estate near Nyon. In summer, he is out in the alpine meadows, which are his specialty and are not confined to the Alps. Many alpages, as the meadows are called, are rented by herdsmen from local communes, which own them. Farmers and their herdsmen are not always assiduous about keeping the alpages in good condition and trim repair. Cattle wander into the trees, where they trample the forests threadbare, and that is most un-Swiss. Agronomists and others study the situation, decide what space should be for meadow and how much space should be for trees. The neat, absolute lines are drawn with subsidized fencing.

La Place de la Concorde Suisse

It is an incidental touch in the appearance of Switzerland, where human beings have coiffed nature at almost every altitude—accomplishing things with respect to the original that, truth be told, are rarely an affront. People who paint pictures that look like Switzerland are put down as simpleminded romantic idealists, whereas they actually belong to the literal-statement and compressed-rusticity school. It is possible that people who prefer landscapes without evidence of mankind have come to prefer them because evidence of mankind is ordinarily so disappointing. While making their artifacts everywhere attractive, the Swiss have not embarrassed their terrain.

If Switzerland is arguably the most beautifully developed landscape in the world, this is so, to some extent, through necessity, because Switzerland is so small; and its size creates a military problem, for Switzerland has much to hide. Thorn and rose, there is scarcely a scene in Switzerland that would not sell a calendar, and—valley after valley, mountain after mountain, village after village, page after page—there is scarcely a scene in Switzerland that is not ready to erupt in fire to repel an invasive war. "About this we don't talk," a colonel on the general staff said to me one day. "Don't ask me about it. But keep your eyes open. You may see something."

One does not have to be trained by the Central Intelligence Agency to see the airstrips like Band-Aids all over the Alps. There is no attempt to conceal them. No one is suggesting they are Autobahns that ran rapidly out of funds. Like the hangars within the mountains, further installations are more subtle. In forests are many clearings that seem to make no sense. On calendars, they would appear to be alpages. But there are no cows, no chalets, no herdsmen—and no one cuts a tree in Switzerland without a federal permit. Why, then, the patches of clear-cut woods? They are fields of fire. Hidden in the rock behind them are extremely modern cannons trained on something—the mouth of a tunnel, a pier of a bridge —that might need the instant attention of prepared fire. All calculations are long since logged, and the shells are ready to fly. Thousands of big guns are emplaced in the rock of Switzerland, and, to an extent that is secret, are continuously manned. On the road to Simplon Pass, above Brig—about ten kilometres from the sector of Massy's patrol—a new bridge stands on slim rectangular pillars more than four hundred feet above a wide gorge: a curving bridge, of white concrete with concealed suspension cables, lovely to behold, veering through space, an engineering masterwork. It has shortened and simplified the route over Simplon, and, Simplon being what it is, there can be no doubt that the Swiss are ready to dynamite the bridge at any moment, including this instant. The system of demolition is routinely practiced. Often, in such assignments, the civilian engineer who created the bridge will, in his capacity as a military officer, be given the task of planning its destruction. Once it is destroyed, it must stay destroyed, so there is need for covering fire. The Simplon road, traversing many cliffs, offers so much spectacle that people in automobiles tend not to study the stone in the retaining walls. It is block granite, or something like it, and in places the texture is a little off. One such place is two kilometres north of the high curving bridge. There is no stopping, no shoulder there beside the road, but if you pull off into the recesses of the next avalanche shed and walk back you see on close inspection that some of the granite is plastic. A couple of dozen plastic-granite blocks form two removable squares. In effect, they are windows—closed for the season. They look directly at the near end of the bridge. Prepared fire. "Don't ask me about that. But keep your eyes open. You may see something."

To interrupt the utility of bridges, tunnels, highways, railroads, Switzerland has established three thousand points of demolition. That is the number officially printed. It has been suggested to me that to approximate a true figure a reader ought to multiply by two. Where a highway bridge crosses a railroad, a segment of the bridge is programmed to drop on the railroad. Primacord fuses are built into the bridge. Hidden artillery is in place on either side, set to prevent the enemy from clearing or repairing the damage. All purposes included, concealed and stationary artillery probably number upward of twelve thousand guns. The Porcupine Principle. Near the German border of Switzerland, every railroad and highway tunnel has been prepared to pinch shut explosively. Nearby mountains have been made so porous that whole divisions can fit inside them. There are weapons and soldiers under barns. There are cannons inside pretty houses. Where Swiss highways happen to run on narrow ground between the edges of lakes and the bottoms of cliffs, man-made rockslides are ready to slide.

Through locked gates you see corridors in the sides of mountains—going on and on into the rock, with a light in the ceiling every five metres and far too many to count. There are general hospitals inside mountain rock. There is stored petroleum—at least enough to fuel the completely mobilized army for more than a year, from the first jet aircraft to the last Haflinger. There is food, of course, and, needless to add, munitions. All these things have shelf lives and are regularly sold or otherwise used, while fresh materials are added. There is a Swiss Army bread that lasts two years. It is vacuum-packed and hard as rock. When exposed to air, it swells and softens. Munitions are hidden also in forests. Captains know where they are.

Various countries spy on Swiss defenses and attempt to diagram the hidden installations—including the Soviet Union, whose mapping project in Switzerland has not escaped the notice of the Swiss. The Russians obviously regard armed neutrality as a charming paper phrase. They associate Switzerland with the North Atlantic Treaty Organization, even if Switzerland protestingly does not. The Russians appear to look upon Switzerland as a kind of capitalist Alamo—a likely position of ultimate defense for a falling Western Europe.

Riding around Switzerland with these matters in mind—seeing little driveways that blank out in mountain walls, cavern entrances like dark spots under mountainside railroads and winding corniches, portals in various forms of lithic disguise—you can find it difficult not to imagine that almost anything is a military deception, masking a hidden installation. You see the big closed doors of a building that appears to be a garage for snowplows. But why would snowplows need to be surrounded by such a high fence and so much barbed wire? Possibly they plow snow with ten-and-a-half-centimetre cannons. Possibly the building is something like the top of a mine shaft. Not all underground installations are entered through the sides of mountains. Some are entered through ordinary buildings and basements—and spread out far underground. You see a mountain, quite able to retain its own sides, with a huge wall of concrete set into its base, apparently doorless, windowless—blank. Elsewhere, you see talus, and when you look up to see the mountain that shed it there is no mountain. You infer that such material came from somewhere, and sense the vastness of underground spaces by the volume of the broken rock.

There are three defense centers, each almost wholly concealed, that are known as fortresses—one near the Austrian frontier, another at the head of Lake Geneva, and the third in the region of Saint Gotthard, the central Alpine pass. The fortresses have been likened to underground ant colonies, and they are continuously manned. While soldiers like Massy and Wettstein patrol the valleys and the hills to satisfy refresher courses, others in the militia spend the same time underground. The fortresses are somewhat misnamed—Festungen, forteresses—for the word seems to imply a unitary citadel, a Fort Ticonderoga by the shore of Lake Champlain, when in fact the fortresses are networks of tunnels, caverns, bunkers, and surface installations, each spread through many tens of square miles. Supplementing the fortresses is a much more widely distributed system of redoubts—rock-defended installations of related character, some of even greater size. The dimensions, sites, and purposes of all these defenses are secret even within the army—known only to those who need to know. Ironically, some of them were built with the help of foreign workers, who know where they are, while Swiss do not.

Switzerland seems to be ready for any invader—red, black, yellow, or white.

"We are going to be neutral, and whoever wants to come in here and make use of our territory, in action against us or a third state, we will kick him out."

"It's not playing, what we do."

"We are quite ready. The basic Christian idea is: I smash you; you turn and say, 'Smash here also.' The Swiss are not going to do that."

"In the Second World War, the will to defend was absolutely there. That will is very much unbroken."

The speakers are Swiss colonels, majors, and captains. The dialogue consists of fragments assembled from visits here and there.

"In Switzerland, there are people prepared to fight even against the government if the government were to capitulate."

"We dislike war. We don't want war. We must be

so impressive that the war never starts. I'm not sure we can do that. But I hope we can."

"Ten per cent of the people of Switzerland are in the Swiss Army. If ten per cent of the people in the United States were in a Volks army, it would include twenty-two million personnel. Think of the impression *that* would make on the Russians. An army is always a matter of impression, isn't it?"

"Even if we are subjected to nuclear blackmail, we will never give up."

Within all these remarks lies the essential nuance of the Swiss idea of neutrality—the essential nuance being brute military power. The Swiss definition of neutrality absolutely includes an army, because the task of a neutral country is to defend its territory. Switzerland's declaration of independence is that it will attack no one, will participate in no so-called police action, will make no alliance, and will defend itself. In a book subtitled "La Suisse en Armes" is a picture of a small boy beside a large cannon under a camouflage net, with the caption "Pour rester libre, un peuple libre a besoin de canons." Bumper stickers on Swiss cars say:

TOUS PARLENT AU SUJET DE LA PAIX
NOTRE ARMÉE L'A PRÉSERVÉE

"You have to be strong defensively to be neutral. Our population density and our terrain make armed neutrality possible."

"You need trumps, and the Alpine passes are our trumps."

"The Swedish are as aggressively neutral as we are.

They spend a lot of money on their army. But they have a lot of land. It is doubtful that they could defend it."

"Japan could do it. But they have too many people. With a hundred and seventeen million people, they will soon fall off the islands. And then what will they do? They will spread out into the Pacific again."

Switzerland—sixty per cent alpine—has a fistful of trumps. And altogether the Swiss national periphery is a natural defense. The high Alps, of course, form the southern and eastern frontiers, while the northern and western borders are largely defined by the Jura—a range of older and gentler mountains—and by two considerable lakes: Lake Geneva, also known as Lac Léman, and Lake Constance, the Bodensee. The Jura is so thoroughly prepared that it suggests a beached and camouflaged battleship. While attack could come from anywhere, it is anticipated from the northeast. When an officer sketches a map of basic national strategy, like as not he will draw an arrow coming in from that direction, and he might say, "That is the main assumption. Because we are neutral, we are not allowed to say that—but that is the assumption."

Within its natural shell, the army's initial mode of defense is to make clear that anyone who wants to travel aggressively through central Europe might find it advisable to avoid Switzerland.

"The invader sees the type of army we have, the density of the troops—and decides it is not worthwhile to invade. Then we have done something."

If deterrence fails, the border country is defended everywhere by contiguous embunkered brigades—soldiers in the thirty-three-to-forty-two age group who regularly train in the same places and collectively know every tree. There is some debate about Basel. It is Switzerland's second-largest city, and an industrial treasure, but it lies beyond the Jura—so close to Germany that one of its railway stations is a part of the German rail network, and passengers have to go through German customs in order to board a train, and so close to France that people at one chemical and pharmaceutical firm (Sandoz) have to go through French customs to get to the company tennis courts. How is anybody going to defend that?

"In the center of Basel, you can defend a few houses; otherwise, forget it."

"You can blow up the Rhine bridges. That's about all. Basel could not be defended."

"While Lake Geneva, the Alps, Lake Constance, the Rhine, and the Jura circumscribe Switzerland, Basel is out in the cold."

"Basel? Undefendable? Just try coming in here. You don't want to come into a town like this with a mechanical army. It would be rather nasty."

Given Basel's apparent vulnerability, it is worthy of note that the army is constantly there. The army is not conceding an inch of Switzerland. In the rush-hour twilight of a November day, I was walking across the Rhine on the Mittlere Brücke when half a dozen soldiers in combat camouflage ran onto the bridge with a very long wire and inserted it in a hole. From time to time, a head popped up through the hole. Passersby scarcely seemed to notice all this. Bridge-blowing practice is quite routine in Basel.

After the enemy seizes Basel, and overwhelms or bypasses the defenders of the Jura, the next several lines of resistance have been drawn in the Mittelland. Lying between mountains, the rectangular center of Switzerland is as rich as a chocolate bar and about as easily consumed. In a nation renowned as dairyland, it is the creamiest country that God has ever seen. It is the billowing, stream-dissected plateau country of Gruyère, of the Emmental, of the Lake of the Four Forest Cantons. It contains most of the Swiss population, most of the nation's wealth and industry. It contains Bern, Lucerne, Zurich, Winterthur. Switzerland has three entire army corps in the Mittelland alone. The corps de campagne, as they are known, consist almost wholly of élite troops, which is to say young ones. Strategically, to slow an enemy there is not much to blow up in the Mittelland; but the corps de campagne are highly mobile, mechanized, flexible, and extensively practiced in flame-throwing, grenade-tossing, bullet-spattering house-to-house combat.

"The price for a Russian invader is quite high. Even the Mittelland is bad for mechanized troops—so many houses, towns, rivers, so much population density. The topography is vulnerable, but the civil infrastructure is a defense in itself. You can't fight a big mechanized battle there."

The Mittelland is nevertheless about as vulnerable as Basel. And it presents a strategic paradox. The army is better off in the mountains. The people are better off with the army. During the Second World War, when the planned strategy was to leave the Mittelland open and defend the Alps, many citizens of the Mittelland spent the war in the mountains. The strategy now is to defend the Mittelland with troops that are prepared and equipped to pull back rapidly into the Alps. There are at present no plans for withdrawing the civilian population to the mountains, but in significant numbers that would certainly happen.

"The army can't very well defend mountains and leave people behind."

In July of 1940, when General Guisan convoked his commandants on the meadow where Switzerland, in 1291, was formed, he spoke of "the natural force of our country, the incomparable possibilities for resistance offered to us by our terrain, rich in obstacles and cover, our mountains above all." He called the Alps invincible, and the people who have succeeded him echo what he said.

"We are sure we have a fair chance, because of the specialities of our country. We can easily block an attack. Where there are not mountains, there is water on every side. Someone who attacks us has to cross it. We have a very strong infrastructure in the mountains. We have a good chance that no one will attack us, because the price he has to pay is too high."

"The Alps are younger and less eroded than, say, the Rocky Mountains. There is less level ground among them. Thus, they are an even greater obstacle."

"In the mountains, mechanization doesn't help you any. You are almost lost with armored cars."

"The Gotthard freeway can be protected by ten men. This is exactly what you see in Afghanistan. The Russians cannot deal with that except by getting out of their armored cars."

If the enemy were to come into the Alps, they would encounter still another army corps—including Soldat Wettstein, Soldat Massy, Lieutenant Wyssa, Major Hentsch, Divisionnaire Tschumy, and the Tenth Mountain Division. In rough outline, the idea in the mountains is to blow up every point of access to the regional fortresses, so that armed forces—friendly or hostile—can go in and out only by helicopter. Needless to say, the demolition is ready.

"Don't forget: this is not the Plain of the Schleswig-Holstein. Our terrain is prepared for destruction, and then it defends itself."

And what if it does not?

"Our lines of defense are deep—one, two, three, four, five, six, seven. If all lines are penetrated, if the enemy comes into the Alps, guerrilla warfare follows."

And what then? Perhaps it would be apposite to ask a foreign military strategist rather than a Swiss—Switzerland's defenses being less than unknown to people in other armies.

"I personally would hate to have to go in there and dig them out. It would take a tremendous amount of force to peel them out of those god-damned mountains. For anyone who wants to go in there, the cost would be very high; and it would be even more expensive to stay in. They all know how to shoot, and shoot well. They would fight tooth and nail. They know their country like the back of their hand. And remember: theirs is a different mission from ours or most armies'. They do not have to be trained to fight in deserts or malarial swamps, to chase an enemy out of one physiographic world and into another. Their mission is to defend Switzerland. It is all defensive. They are a strong armed force —amazingly well trained for a country that hasn't been in a war for hundreds of years."

Luc Massy shifts his rifle on its strap and ventilates himself by unsnapping his jacket. "If war came, I don't think we would resist very long," he says. "But the army is very good for unemployment. When the army comes, many people in the villages are working."

"To defend Switzerland from the mountains is a myth," Jean-Bruno Wettstein says. "No enemy will come into the Alps. The population is in the Mittelland, and we have nothing to defend here but rocks, snow, and téléphériques. As a soldier, as a citizen, I really don't understand the possibilities of the Swiss Army. Given what I know of other countries and their armies, I don't think we can defend Switzerland."

"We may not have a very big chance, but as long as we have a small chance it is useful to do it," says Massy.

Wettstein replies, "If you put ten divisions of Russian

tanks in Basel, they won't take too much time to arrive in Geneva."

The patrol has walked several kilometres on the high ground above the Rhone and now looks down on the Nussbaum bridge. The drop is steep at first, through a meadowful of agile cows, and then considerably steeper. Massy, chef de patrouille, cannot see a way to go down, and neither can anyone else. Massy looks west, studying possibilities. Massy looks east. Massy looks down at his boots and past his toes to the Nussbaum bridge. What to do? The hour is somewhat past noon. The sun at last is bathing the deep narrow valley. The breeze is becoming warm. The larches are bright gold. The meadow is dry. The bridge can wait. When in doubt, eat lunch.

We sit down and break out our Valais bread and cheese. Across the valley, a waterfall erupts from dark wooded slopes of the Bettmeralp, which is treeless and white far above. Near the waterfall, a dark-brown village clings to the alp. Over our heads, an eagle is sliding through the sky. Massy removes from his pack a bulky towel and unrolls it to reveal a bottle of wine. In his battle jacket he keeps a tire-bouchon, always ready, like a grenade. He opens its knife blade and deroofs the leaded wine. He erects the corkscrew and revolves it into the cork. He sets the lever arm on the lip of the bottle. We hear the sound of a tennis ball, well hit. Massy runs the cork by his nose. In his breast pocket, at all times, is a small plastic cylinder that resembles a dice cup. It protects a drinking glass so small that even in its sheath it does not create a bulge in the jacket. With straight, converging sides, it has the simple shape of a peach basket, if not the size. It holds six centilitres and is a verre de cave, a winemaker's glass, whose proportions any Swiss winemaker could identify as the glass of the Canton de Vaud.

Massy fills the glass, holds it up to his eye. "Santé," he says, with a nod to the rest of us, and—thoughtfully, unhurriedly—drinks it himself. Because I happen to be sitting beside him on his left, he says, "John, you are not very well placed. In my town, we drink counterclockwise." After finishing the glass, he fills it again and hands it to his right—to Jean Reidenbach. The background music is a dissonance of cattle bells. We count nineteen Brown Swiss in the meadow just below us, and they sound like the Salvation Army. A narrow red train appears far below. Coming out of a tunnel, it crosses a bridge, whistling—three cars in all, the Furka-Oberalp. The train will go up the Rhone until there is no more Rhone, and then climb on cogs to the Furka Pass, and the Oberalp Pass, to finish its journey descending the nascent Rhine, pool to cascade pool, pastel green with glacial flour. The railroad bridge is a beautiful stonework that looks like a piece of a cloister. In all respects but width, it shames the Nussbaum bridge, the latter being wide enough for two automobiles or possibly one red tank. A téléphérique is down there as well. We are too high to see trout. Wires go up the Bettmeralp. Denis Schyrr volunteers to get the necessary facts at the téléphérique station later on, but he adds, "Do you suppose they speak French?"

Massy shrugs. He takes the glass from Reidenbach, refills it, and hands it to Schyrr. "This is a good way to drink," Massy remarks. "A good way to avoid getting —you know—drunk." Six centilitres is about two ounces. If the glass were filled with whiskey, you would know you'd had a drink. The apples and sausages are fresh and good, less so the pâté in the can. The sunlight is delicious. The packs are supportive. The rifles lean against a tree. After Pierre Pera, it is my turn to drink, and then Massy's, Reidenbach's, Schyrr's, Wettstein's, Pera's, mine, and Massy's. Pera is a plumber in Montreux. Denis Schyrr, blond and scholarly with his metal-rimmed spectacles, is a landscape gardener, a paysagiste-horticulteur, in La Tour de Peilz, near Vevey. Jean Reidenbach, with his tall rustic frame and unruly hair, looks like some sort of paysagiste himself, but is in fact a receptionist at the Ramada in Geneva. The wine is light and pleasant, not to say elegant. Massy pours himself another measure and contemplates it against the Bettmeralp, gold on white. From the one bottle, it is amazing how many times the glass will go around. It stops where it stops—even if the ritual ends, as it always begins, with Massy. Fraternité—yes. Égalité—no. Last month in Lausanne, at the Concours de Jean-Louis, Massy placed sixth in a field of ten thousand wine tasters. Here in this Valais meadow, the label on the bottle in his hand says "Clos du Boux, Epesses. J.-F. Massy, Propriétaire." J.-F. is Massy's father, now his partner, who is trim, compact, has an aquiline nose, and—including the bemused smile —looks exactly like Massy. Also on the label is a line drawing of a two-story house with a Bernese roof, Lombardy poplars at each end. It is completely surrounded by the vines of the Clos du Boux. The house consists of two ground floors, affixed to the slanting vineyard. Massy lives downstairs with his wife and infant son. His father and his mother live above. He leans on his pack and in the balmy sunlight closes his eyes. Three days ago, he was in Epesses making wine.

The cave was a ganglion of hoses and tubes: Massy fixing leaks with surgical cotton, Massy on a ladder with a light bulb and a cord, Massy inside the cuves. He was wearing high rubber boots, bluejeans, and a rubber apron over a cotton football shirt bearing the number "26" and the name "BROWNS." He was racking a new white—in its taste a hint of something foul. Time had come to separate the wine from its lees. The ladder was leaning against the tiled wall of a cuve—a tall and narrow chamber full of wine. On the outside of the cuve, a column of wine in a clear-plastic tube reported the depth inside. In this cave were twenty-one cuves, also a big oak cask—in all, a hundred and thirty-five thousand litres of wine. Massy was working alone. He was working like a soldier. With a hose that could have put out a fire, he sent most of the contents of a cuve into an aeration tub, where it spilled like a fountain into a foaming pool and by another hose was sucked away. The wine was not at all attractive. It looked like floodwater, like weak tea with skim milk in it, like something a chemical company had decided to hide. Sometimes he was interrupted by people who came to the cave to buy the product from the oenologist himself. Between rackings, he might have a few moments to sit and read *La Tribune du Matin*, but scarcely enough time to turn a page. He was racking at the rate of thirty-two thousand litres a day. Now and again, he picked up something that looked like a flamethrower and shot needles of cold water with steamlike force over the walls and floor of the cave. "If you are clean—if everything that touches the wine is clean—it is easy to make wine," he said. From time to time, he would pick up a small hose and let a slow downbending stream of wine fall past his tongue until he found the moment where the quality stopped. When a cuve was drawn down and its wine transferred, he opened a small oak door at the bottom and mucked out the offensive lees. They came forth like a warm coffee ice cream that had begun to sour. Putting on a yellow rain slicker, an impermeable yellow hat, Massy then crawled inside the cuve. If odor could kill, he would have fallen dead. He hosed out the interior. This had been a most unusual year, he said from inside —his voice distorted, tympanic, echoing, fermenting. He said he would be making about a hundred and seventy thousand litres—a volume approaching twice his annual average. There had been a fine spring, a better summer, with ample but not excessive rain. "Also," he added, "for four years the vines have not given much."

The door of the cuve was so small that a larger man could not have gone through it. It had the circumference of an oval placemat. After Massy came out, he lined the edges with beeswax, replaced the oak, and tried to secure it with a bolt. He had repeated trouble with the thread of the bolt. Minutes went by while he could not make it tight. "Losing time!" he shouted out in his frustration. "Losing time for Massy! Merde!" The soldier who would soon be joking in the mountains was someone else in the cave.

The cave was the basement of a building with thick stone walls, tall oak doors, and blue shutters, on the main thoroughfare of Epesses, a street so intimate that red and green lights forced the traffic to move in one direction at a time. Epesses was the sort of town that could stop a tour bus like a cork in a bottle. Two bicycles would have had difficulty passing in the Ruelle du Vieux Bourg, where the facing eaves of houses all but touched. On the walls there, and all over town, were grapevines and ivy, geraniums and roses, in vigorous color so late in the fall. Springwater poured into stone fountains from spigots set in the walls. Three hundred and sixty people live in Epesses, and if they step outdoors they are leaving town. All around the village are paths among the grapes. The paths run between stone walls and are decorated with stern advice: "DÉFENSE DE PRENDRE DU RAISIN." Also between stone walls, a small stream tumbles into town, passes through Massy's winery, and falls white and cascading to Lac Léman. The vineyards, leaning back from the water, collect the African sun.

Just the one house—Massy's, with its four chimneys (each with a tiled roof), its oak timbers, its balcony of beams and posts—stands apart from the town, suggesting a certain preeminence. It has been there for three hundred years, a long curving structure convex to the view

—across the village rooftops to the lake far below and the Savoy Alps beyond. Epesses is the ancestral village of Divisionnaire Tschumy. It is the village also of Eric Dessemontet, a vintner who has achieved the rank of captain and commands the company in which Massy serves. Vineyards are measured in fossoriers—an ancient reckoning of the amount of ground that could be worked by one man in a day. In the Lavaux wine region, of which Epesses is a part, an average winemaking family has thirty fossoriers. Dessemontet has twenty-eight. The Massys have a hundred and seventy. Protestant refugees, they came to Switzerland from France when the Edict of Nantes was revoked. They made watches for a time, and then wine. They have been soldiers for centuries, too, and now, despite the pressures of the great vendange, it was time for Luc to hang up his hoses and get out his gun.

In the trunk of his white Lancia he put his automatic rifle, his sealed container of bullets, his steel helmet, his various bottles of vin militaire. The football shirt disappeared and was replaced by his dress uniform, in Switzerland's dark sea green. That Swiss soldiers keep weapons and bullets and gas masks at home is one of the open details of rapid mobilization—a procedure that is for the most part classified. To the elemental question "Is your army ready to fight?" a member of the Swiss Army general staff will quickly answer, "Oh, yes, and we don't want to talk about that." All soldiers know their mobilization points and have been told not to reveal where they are. They have been told to go there by any means—on foot, if necessary. If they stop passing cars, the drivers transport them. The soldiers are supposed to carry food and drink for two days. In 1977, a

Swiss brigadier (one star) was sent to prison for eighteen years for giving secrets of mobilization to the Russians. Mobilization begins with an invisible process whereby certain strategic components normally found in concentration are systematically spread out. Partial mobilization, being more difficult than general mobilization, is more frequently practiced. In either situation, soldiers go from mobilization points to assembly areas to alert or battle positions.

All in forty-eight hours?

"That is rather long. If we start in the morning, we would be mobilized by late afternoon. That is why the gun is at home, the ammunition at home. The younger people all have automatic rifles. They are ready to fight."

In the thirteenth century, the confederating peasants kept their weapons at home. The sword became a symbol of their right to vote. In Appenzell, men still carry swords when they turn out to vote.

There are six hundred thousand assault rifles in Swiss homes. It is said that this is a very good thing, for while a father cleans his rifle at the kitchen table his son is watching, and "the boy gets close to the weapon." Communist Swiss soldiers keep rifles and machine guns at home. It is said that this is not dangerous for political purposes; it is dangerous only for the wife. Ammunition boxes are sealed. If the seal is not intact when a soldier returns to duty, serious punishment follows.

On Swiss highways, portable blinking signs appear from time to time, showing certain truck drivers where to turn and go in practice mobilization. When a Swiss citizen buys a truck, the registration may carry a notice that the truck will be taken over by the government in time of war. Not all Swiss trucks are included—just the percentage needed. The owners have no choice.

After a last look around the cave and a chat of farewell with his family, Massy got into his Lancia and drove east on the Route du Vignoble—La Corniche de Lavaux —from village to village halfway up the lake slope, with tens of thousands of vines below him and tens of thousands above, terraced by retaining walls. He said the underlying rock was limestone, forever feeding nutrients to the soil. He said the reflection coming off the lake is particularly strong around Epesses and is known as the second sun. The retaining walls are unusually high, and they keep the sun's heat and warm the vines at night. "The berries go on ripening even in the dark."

On a street in Montreux, he picked up Gilles Fantony, a friend he sees only in the army. An ordinary soldier, like Massy, Fantony is the Swiss equivalent of a stockbroker, employed by the Union Bank of Switzerland. Over the past three weeks, he had grown a beard, so that he would not have to shave while in the army.

The Lancia proceeded along the lakeshore, and at Chillon the road became confined to an extremely narrow space between a cliff and the water—a perfect place to blow up, to cover with prepared fire. Even Lord Byron might have noted that. Just by the road, and partly in the lake, stood the Castle of Chillon, where for five centuries every kind of firearm known to man had been set to stop anything that moved. Opposite the castle was fake stonework, concealing the artillery behind it.

The highway soon became dual, and, approaching Saint-Maurice, had a divider made of cables, light-alloy posts, and wire mesh. Massy remarked that the posts were

42

removable, from sleeves embedded in the concrete, and in a matter of minutes a few kilometres of divider could be carried to the side of the road. This is practiced at least once a year. From concealed bunkers, jets appear, roar up the highway, pass under bridges, rise into the sky.

At Saint-Maurice—epicenter of the western fortress, protector of the Valais, bastion of the Upper Rhone—the topography tightens, mountains draw close on both sides of the river, and the patterns of preset artillery fire probably resemble tartan.

"Je suis papa," said Massy. He had neglected to mention to Fantony that he had become a parent since his last course in the army.

"Félicitations!" said Fantony.

"Un garçon!" said Massy.

Fantony clapped his hands, applauding the brilliant performance.

Around Saint-Maurice, the Rhone Valley was essentially without vines, because the river runs north there and the slopes do not face the sun. At Martigny, however, the river, the road, and the entire landscape made a ninety-degree turn to the east, and now the prodigious vineyards of Valais were spread up the south-facing slopes. Out there in front of us we saw very high mountains, too, and Massy thought the snow line looked uncomfortably low. "Ai," he said. "The snow is too close. Two or three times, we will sleep outside."

"Perhaps we will not have to go so high."

"There will be rain below. These boots are not good in rain. They pump water."

The valley floor was three kilometres wide and as

flat as the lake bed it became when the ice melted. Apples, pears, cherries, the flatland was covered with orchards. The mountains went up steeply, like the sides of Massy's glass. The glacier had not been uniformly successful in cutting off the mountains' spurs, and where they had resisted strongly the big valley now and again seemed to pinch itself closed. Falling rock, in great quantity, had formed obstacles, too. Deep gorges broke the sides. It was wiser to enter this valley in a white Lancia than in a red tank.

There were towers of isolate rock standing in the valley—two at Sion, one at Raron—each supporting a castle or a church. James Fenimore Cooper preferred these rock eminences to the Acropolis: "The Acropolis does not overhang Athens in a more kingly style, than these rocks frown upon the humbler town of Sion, nor do I believe that the architecture of the former, however pure and classical, is half as picturesque." Cooper, travelling through here a hundred and fifty years ago, was even less attracted to the mountains than the shivering Massy. Cooper noted that the rock was "stern" and "naked," and that the mountains were "streaked with sterility."

Massy was in less than a hurry to report for active duty. His way of going into the army was to stop off at vineyards and call on friends—classmates, in effect, from Montagibert, the federal school for oenologists and viticulteurs. He stopped and toured a cave or two. He toured the Domaine du Mont d'Or, near Sion. In an atmosphere dreamy with the nose-tingling smell of fermentation, he looked at inflatable rubber presses and browsed over the labels in the company's Vinothèque. A sign above the bottles pleaded: "NE NOUS TOUCHEZ PAS! NOUS DORMONS!"

More wine comes out of Sion than any other place in the country, he remarked as we drove on up the road. Now the terraces on the valleyside reminded me of the football stadium at the University of Texas, where the side that holds the home crowd rises tier upon tier until people are seated in the sky. Switzerland produces about a hundred million litres a year, and consumes virtually all of it. Moreover, Switzerland imports two-thirds of what it drinks. Switzerland imports more Beaujolais than is imported by the United States. Dôle is the predominant red wine of the Valais, and the white is called Fendant. In my opinion, Fendant is guzzling-good wine. To compare it with his own, Massy extended himself to the limits of his generosity, saying, "Fendant will have less character, and be heavier, so you can drink one or two bottles, but maybe not more." Massy worked a season in the Napa Valley, attempting to expand his knowledge. Among the things he learned was that if you put wood chips in wine it will taste of oak.

At Turtmann, we passed a long airstrip, and five twin-boom jet Venoms happened to be emerging like lobsters from holes in the lateral rock. As jet fighters go, Venoms are something less than state of the art. They are used for instruction. "Would you believe it?" said Massy. "Those planes are partly made of wood."

The traffic—military trucks, cars, and to some extent the Venoms, too—was being delayed by a woman leading a herd of cows. She was riding a motorcycle and wearing a steel helmet.

The journey was almost over, the car approaching Brig. I mentioned to Massy that I had been told that Swiss militiamen could scarcely wait to get back into the army—that they looked forward to it from one year to the next. "Not everyone thinks alike," he said. "I do it because I have to, and because I think I can help a little bit—also to be equal with the others who do it." He went on to say that the "obsession" of most soldiers during basic training was not to be chosen to become a corporal and therefore possibly an officer. "It's O.K. for people in bureaus, but if you have your own proper business it's not. To be a captain is to spend almost two months of your year each year." He repeated that he was busy at home, the clouds looked unfriendly, and he could do without the cold mountain air. The clouds had spread out to reveal even higher peaks, like long gray razors scraping lather. "It is cold here," he complained. "Oh! It is cold." We had come into the outskirts of the small, medieval city where the Simplon Tunnel goes into the rock. Brig: where the Furka-Oberalp intersects the national railroad, where the highway ascends toward Italy, where a large part of the Fifth Regiment had been told to arrive at noon. At eleven-fifty-five, Massy drew into a parking slot at the railway station. Far up the platforms, all over the streets, everywhere we looked were soldiers. They filled up the station house, the Second Class Buffet, the booths in the postal telephone. We got out of the car. Massy buttoned his tunic. He cinched the leather belt around his waist. "Voilà," he said. "We're in the army now."

It seems likely that the two most widely circulated remarks ever made about Switzerland's military prowess were made by Napoleon Bonaparte and Orson Welles.

Welles said, "In Italy for thirty years under the Borgias, they had warfare, terror, murder, bloodshed—but they produced Michelangelo, Leonardo da Vinci, and the Renaissance. In Switzerland, they have brotherly love, five hundred years of democracy and peace, and what did that produce? The cuckoo clock."

Napoleon said, "The best troops—those in whom you can have the most confidence—are the Swiss."

Welles spoke his lines in "The Third Man," a motion picture that deservedly attracted an extensive worldwide audience. The screenplay was written by Graham Greene, who later published the preliminary treatment in book form, but Greene was not the author of the lines about the Borgias and Switzerland. They were interpolated by the ingenious Welles, who may have chosen to suppress in his memory the fact that when Italy was enjoying the Borgias, Switzerland was enjoying a reputation as—to quote Douglas Miller's "The Swiss at War"—"the most powerful and feared military force in Europe." Switzerland was about as neutral in those days as had been Mongolia under Genghis Khan. Not only were the Swiss ready to fight. They fought. They had a militia system that could mobilize fifty-four thousand soldiers. They knew enough warfare and bloodshed to sicken a Borgia. They were so chillingly belligerent that even if they were destroyed in battle they had been known in the same moment to win a war. One afternoon in mid-Renaissance, a few hundred Swiss who were outnumbered fifteen to one elected not to run away but to wade across a river and break into the center of the opposition, where all of them died, but not before they had slaughtered three thousand of their French enemies. The French Army was so unnerved that it struck its tents and fled.

It was the Swiss who unhorsed the mounted knight, and in a sense their confederation—their Everlasting League—was formed with that in mind. The peasants of the forest cantons made their pact of mutual defense because they wished not to be the vassals of alien equestrian lords. They waited twenty-four years for the first big test of their ability to resist—ample time to be prepared, to rehearse what they would do. Then, in 1315, two thousand Austrian knights appeared, leading a considerable army, and fatally attempted to make use of Morgarten pass. The knights were aristocrats, accustomed to tournament warfare and not to peasants attacking them from higher ground. The peasants came down on them with tree trunks, halberds, axes, and plummeting rock. The pass was blocked. The horses and riders became compressed and hopelessly jammed. The peasants rushed among them and hacked them down. Few knights survived. ("In the mountains, mechanization doesn't help you any. You are almost lost with armored cars.")

Also in the Renaissance, Swiss soldiers began sewing white crosses on their doublets, so they would recognize one another in the confusion of infantry battle. When mounted knights attacked them in open country, the Swiss formed squares—ten thousand soldiers in a square, bristling with twenty-one-foot pikes: the Porcupine Principle. In the course of time, they developed some interesting equipment. They developed the Lucerne hammer, fundamentally a poleaxe with a brass fist on its head and spikes protruding between the fingers. They developed the Morgenstern, an eight-foot cudgel with a sixteen-spike pineapple head. And they developed the Swiss Army knife.

Its precursor was a simple fifteenth-century dagger that every warrior carried. Over a hundred years, it acquired so many additions and complications that only officers and rich citizens could afford it, and it fell into disuse. It was an infantry weapon, but in its advanced stages it acquired built-in forks and other utensils. Competition waxed in the decorating of sheaths with scroll ornaments in gold and silver, and expensive foreign artists—such as the Hans Holbeins—were employed to do the work. The knife every soldier is issued today is jacketed with quilted gray aluminum, has one blade, a

49

can opener, a bottle opener, a hole punch, two screw-drivers, and no corkscrew. On one side is a small red shield bearing the white cross. The knife is made identically by two companies—Victorinox and Wenger—that also make the red knives that in commercial display cases are all stuck apart like swastikas and include fish disgorgers, ski-wax scrapers, international wrenches, magnifying glasses, tweezers, toothpicks, scissors, and saws. The gray army knife resembles the simpler of the commercial offerings, minus the red plastic. Officers included, everyone in the Swiss Army carries a Swiss Army knife. Once, at the end of a long session in driving snow with machine guns firing and grenades exploding—up on the high ground where such practice can be conducted with live ammunition—I walked down with the Fifth Regiment's Colonel Marc-Henri Chaudet, and when he reached the roadhead he discovered that his automobile would not start. It was a gray Mercedes-Benz, and—with its hood up—its engine looked even grayer, there in the wind and stinging snow, many miles from the nearest garage and almost as many from the nearest warm room. After six hours of storm weather and steep inclines, the Colonel might have been forgiven if he had displayed exasperation. This, after all, was Switzerland, where everything works; Switzerland, where trains run like clocks, and clocks run like watches, and watches are synchronous with the pulse of the universe; Switzerland, where electric eyes watch underground parking spaces and turn on green lights when they are free; Switzerland, where electric eyes watch urinals and flush not only the one under address but the one next to it as well; Switzer-

land, where switches in mattresses cause rooms to go
dark as people get into bed; and now, in Switzerland,
the Colonel was inconvenienced by this weather-
whipped, tuned-down, one-jewel German car, which
wheezed but would not cough. Colonel Chaudet—a
Vevey lawyer—gave it a cool glance, sighting along his
nose. Tall, slim, handsome—his trousers taut and neatly
creased and disappearing inside his boots like a downhill skier's—the Colonel had a certain downplay in the
corners of his mouth, suggesting, among other things,
detached amusement. Besides, he had complete confidence in his soldiers and their equipment. Observing the
difficulty, a corporal stepped forward, removed from a
pocket his Swiss Army knife, used a fingernail to expose
the can opener, and leaned into the Mercedes. Within
ten minutes, the engine was running.

The Swiss infantry, six hundred years ago, knew
not only how to form a square but also how to break
through almost anything. At Sempach—a name of res-
onance in Switzerland—a soldier named Arnold Winkelried gathered to his body the pike points of many
foemen, thus opening on either side of him holes in the
Austrian line, through which the Swiss backfield poured,
swinging six-foot halberds, while Winkelried died. For
each Swiss who died at Sempach, nine Austrians died as
well, many of them dismounted knights. Machiavelli
called the Swiss "the new Romans." In the Quattro-
cento, exactly three hundred years before the United
States declared its independence, the Swiss won a great
victory at a small town called Morat, defeating Burgun-
dian invaders who were threatening the city of Fribourg.
Among the Swiss ordnance were mortars that shot

chunks of limestone and granite. Four hundred and ten
Swiss died at Morat—and twelve thousand Burgundians.
A durable legend sprang from this battle. To wit: a
Swiss courier-soldier, carrying a linden branch, ran with
the glorious news to Fribourg; all but breathless, he at
last approached the ramparts and the towers of the town,
and passed through the main gate and into the central
square, where anxious Fribourgeois had formed a human
circle—magistrates, priests, women on their knees—in
the center of which the courier gathered his last three
breaths, shouted "Victoire! Victoire! Victoire!" and fell
dead, as later recorded, "la face contre terre." It has been
suggested that this story is not without companionship
in a genre. However that may be, there is an old sick
linden in Fribourg that is thought to have grown from
the branch the runner carried. Each year, in October,
a footrace is run from Morat to Fribourg, and it now
attracts about a hundred thousand spectators and eleven
thousand runners. The race has been held for fifty years,
with runners sometimes preparing for the ordeal by
stretching their minds as well as their muscles—chant-
ing in the streets, "Morat! Morat! Morat!" It doesn't
matter that the distance is four-tenths of a marathon.

Swiss neutrality began in 1515, when the Swiss
were thoroughly beaten by a French Army under François I at Marignano, in what is now Italy. "I have con-
quered those whom only Caesar managed to conquer
before me," said the French king, and his words were
struck in coin. The confederated cantons, by then thirteen, decided to fight thereafter only as mercenaries in
other people's wars. They were a small nation, rustic,
poor—nothing at all like the service-industry and manu-

facturing society we know today—and to embellish their economy they leased their incomparable soldiers. The cantons have always been importantly autonomous, and never more so than in the sixteenth century, when the political bond between Catholics and Protestants was under so much strain. It is unlikely that during the heaviest reverberations of the Reformation a cooperating army could have been assembled from the Protestant and Catholic cantons, and so, regardless of Marignano, neutrality was now less a matter of policy than a de-facto condition of Swiss life. The militia was then, as it has generally remained, cantonal in character. The cantons did the selling of soldiers. The French bought heavily for three hundred years—now twelve thousand Swiss, now seventy thousand Swiss, now a hundred and sixty-three thousand Swiss, depending on the intensity of the problems of France. For all that time, the Compagnie des Cent-Suisses were the personal bodyguards of the French kings. Scarcely had the Swiss soldiers appeared in the French court when the Pope decided that he wanted some, too; and the Pope, of course, still has them, ninety in all—the only vestige of the Swiss mercenaries.

Switzerland is so conscious—not to say proud—of the service of its mercenaries in foreign armies that a château outside Geneva has been refurbished as a Musée des Suisses à l'Étranger. The most eminent mercenary of all was Colonel Louis Pfyffer, Roi des Suisses, who became a Swiss hero by serving four French kings. Jérôme d'Erlach, of Bern, became a Swiss hero as an Austrian field marshal. François Lefort, of Geneva, became a Swiss hero as a Russian general under Peter the

Great, as Viceroy of the Grand Duchy of Novgorod, as President of all the Councils of Russia, and as the creator and Grand Admiral of the Russian Navy. Swiss mercenaries fought for the Scandinavian kingdoms, the Holy Roman Empire, the Netherlands, Prussia, Poland, Lorraine, Saxony, Savoy, Spain. In various battles, they fought on both sides. They served the Doge of Genoa, the King of Naples, the Elector of Brandenburg. For a large unnegotiable discount, they served Napoleon. Later, they became one of the perennially toughest components of the French Foreign Legion. In the Château de Penthes—the Musée des Suisses à l'Étranger—hangs a British Union Jack with a prominently inset Swiss white cross.

Contracts always specified that if Switzerland was attacked the soldiers would go back to Switzerland. All such contracts have been illegal for something over a hundred years. Meanwhile, by 1830 or so, in places like Bière, the militias of the various cantons were getting together to march, to exercise, to perform military legerdemain before people with parasols and uncorked wine, men in top hats chatting with soldiers in uniform attending the beginning of the federal army. Upward of a hundred thousand people will turn out today to watch the army parade and perform. A retired soldier will visit his unit's refresher course like an old college football player returning to watch a practice. Quite voluntarily, several thousand civilian soldiers annually collect for a thirty-kilometre footrace in which they carry packs and rifles. Beneath the long neutrality, there lies what the Swiss describe as "an aptitude for war." It appears to be an appetite as well—sublimated and under close control.

La Place de la Concorde Suisse

The Landesmuseum in Zurich is the Louvre of the toy soldier. In glass cases there, toy soldiers by the ten thousand engage in replica battles. There are eight military museums in La Suisse Romande alone. In Morges, there are displays not only of Swiss military exploits but also of Aztec sacrifices, the Siege of Alesia (52 B.C.), and the Battle of Zama, with elephants. In the rooms the women come and go talking of Saint-Lô.

The money brought home by mercenary soldiers started Switzerland's banks. In the foyer of the Federal Assembly, in Bern, stand sculptures of four Swiss soldiers—one armed with a halberd, one with a pike, and two with broadswords. Through heavy bronze doors is the Bundesplatz, surrounded on three sides exclusively by contiguous banks, and on the fourth by the national capitol. To this day, what gives Swiss banks their special distinction is not their corporate inventiveness, which is on the level of the Marble Savings Bank, of Rutland, Vermont, but their fortresslike security, which is emphasized by the Swiss Army. More often than not, a high-ranking officer in a Swiss bank will also be a high-ranking officer in the army. The foremost banks—the Three Sisters of Swiss banking—are the Schweizerischer Bankverein, the Schweizerische Bankgesellschaft, and the Schweizerische Kreditanstalt, better known around the world as Crédit

Suisse. The general manager of the Bankverein is Major Walter Frehner. The president of the Bankgesellschaft is Colonel Niklaus Senn. The chief executive officer of Crédit Suisse is Colonel Robert Jeker. In contrast to all other countries, there is in Switzerland a positive correlation between military rank and economic leadership generally. Colonel Fritz Gerber is the chairman of the board of Hoffmann–La Roche. Major Louis von Planta is the chairman of the board of Ciba-Geigy. Chemical companies, insurance companies, construction companies are under the command of majors, colonels, brigadiers.

There is nothing honorific about the military service of these men. They spend one day out of ten in the army. They command battalions, regiments, brigades. The army, in addition to all its other functions, has long been considered a first-rate school of business management. A major commands a battalion of eight hundred. It seems absolutely logical to the Swiss that if a man can lead eight hundred people in military service he can lead a department of that size in civilian life. The special training required for a position on the general staff is looked upon as the equivalent of two years at the Harvard Business School. The Bankgesellschaft, like the army, has a series of special schools through which its officers rise in rank: an assistant-vice-president school, a vice-president school, a first-vice-president school. The bankers receive orders telling them where to report to school. If you ask a Swiss banker whether his army service has affected his position in the bank, he will usually say something like "Oh, indeed, yes. Now I have this special staff job because of my position in the army." Of course, some banks (and manufacturing and service companies) are more military-minded than others. On the French side of the country, being a "military head" can actually be a disadvantage. There are at least two bank presidents who march with the rank and file. (Switzerland has more than five hundred banking institutions.) An army captain has told me that he once leaped to his feet because the soldier serving him food was an executive vice-president of the company he worked for in Basel. To be high in business and low in the army is less unusual than the reverse; it is rare, perhaps even difficult, for someone to remain low in business while attaining high status in the army. Some corporations actually insist that their employees pursue the highest achievable military rank. When an important business promotion is reported in the press, the notice might say, typically, "He is thirty-seven years old, is married, has three children, lives in Rapperswil, and is a major in the mountain infantry."

During Robert Jeker's parallel rise from soldier to colonel and from trainee to chief executive officer and president of the executive board of Crédit Suisse, he served fifteen hundred days in the army—an average of fifty days a year for thirty years. To Crédit Suisse, this was something more than a patriotic donation of time; it was also a gain for the bank. "The skills you get in one place help you in the other place," Jeker explained to me one day in his office in Zurich. "In the army, we meet people from every level of the community. We come to understand other professions, other companies, other parts of the country. We make business contacts. It helps that we know these people from the army. We are with them twenty-four hours a day.

We know them better than in business life." He paused, and added, "If this bank is choosing a new manager, military record is not one of the major points, but it is never a disadvantage. It will never be negative that someone has to be away from the bank for military service."

Jeker worked in the United States for two and a half years and regularly went home to serve as a second lieutenant. He worked in Paris, Florence, and Buenos Aires, and yet was enabled to spend enough time in Switzerland to become not only a colonel but also a member of the general staff—promotions that demand a great deal of extra time. "It's usual that you are a member of the army," he said. "If not, a part of your life is missing. When we sit together in private life, we often talk about the army. Your conscience can accept it more thoroughly when you know you will attack no one." A tall straightforward man with a guileless smile, Jeker did not advertise in his manner either his high military station or his civilian status as a supergnome. Taking note that he had spent thirty-five days in the army last year and at the same time had been preparing to assume command of one of the most powerful banks in the world, I asked him what he did for a vacation. Where on earth could he go—where had he most recently been—to get away on his own from both the bank and the army?

"Alaska," he said.

Military service is subsidized by industry in various ways. A soldier in a refresher course gets four Swiss francs a day—not enough to pay for an evening's beer. All the while, however, he is being paid as usual by his civilian company, and the government's reimbursement to the company is only seventy per cent—and, of course, the lost work is irrecoverable. An officer uses company telephones to call all over Switzerland on matters having to do with his military unit. He uses the company Xerox, the company computer, his own and his secretary's time—to an extent that varies in direct proportion to the military-mindedness of the supreme executive. If the supreme executive is a Militärkopf, anything goes and the bill will be paid. If a general-staff officer happens to work for Ciba-Geigy in Summit, New Jersey, Ciba-Geigy will pay his way home to serve.

The higher a man rises in the army, the more of his time—by a very large factor—his company gives, for army time in no way invades vacation time. Everyone in the army has his "Little Book of Service," recording, like a pilot's flying time, his total number of service days, and including bare details of the experience—a military scrapbook in efficient form and of such metaphorical reach in Switzerland that Max Frisch has written a book using its title: "Dienstbüchlein." The basic-training period for everyone is seventeen weeks. During basic training, a number of soldiers are invited to become corporals—an advance that requires a hundred and forty-five extra days. This is what Massy did his best to avoid, and his best was good enough. In thirty years of faithful service, Massy as a plain soldier will record in his "Dienstbüchlein" a grand total approximating three hundred and sixty-five days. Colonel Rainer von Falkenstein—just to choose someone for contrast—has already served thirteen hundred days, is only lightly pushing fifty, and will have recorded nearly two thousand days when he retires. Even before he earned his Ph.D. in chemistry, he had served six hundred and fifty days as a machine gunner—a family tradition. The other six hundred and fifty days—as an army specialist in chemical and nuclear weapons—have come out of his employment at the Sandoz pharmaceutical company. It is all in his "Little Book of Service."

Any rise in rank costs many extra days. Serving them is known as "paying your grade." Corporals with a certain something about them are invited to become lieutenants, and for that they pay two hundred and thirty-six days. After leading a section for a number of three-week refresher courses, a lieutenant may be invited to become a captain, and the price for that is a hundred and sixty-five days—while Massy racks wine. As an oenologist, he has formed the opinion that the wine will not become memorable as a result of his being a major, but it could become insipid. Not everyone who is self-employed takes the same short view. Lawyers find the army an excellent milieu for the development of practice. Salesmen in uniform go right on selling. Schoolteachers, who acquire an essentially fixed status at the outset of their careers, tend to seek in the army the rewards and reassurance of promotion.

Certain captains—described as "a crème-de-la-crème élite"—are invited to become candidates for the general staff, which, as in any army, makes plans, forms strategy, and integrates operations. At least five separate courses must be passed to achieve the distinction, and so much additional service that the days are difficult to count. Doctors, lawyers drop aside; they haven't the time. Corporations underwrite the general staff. The exact number of general-staff officers is classified but is something like two thousand. If a corporation has in its hierarchy fifty military officers, possibly two will be on the general staff. There is, of course, no published list. One cannot look these people up. But—Jeker, Heusser, Hupfauf, Bührle—being on the general staff is not a personal secret. A man would list it on his résumé. It is said that a corporation expects fifty per cent more of a member of the general staff, even if he is away eight weeks a year. To perform an exercise all night in rain and then get ready for sleep only to be called out again for some hours and then denied sleep again in order to confront a new situation—and so on for fifty-six consecutive hours—is to undergo training for the general staff. "It was the most stressful time of my life. I would do it again. You are under pressure. You have to make decisions. You are alone. You have to learn. It is good executive training. It is more rigorous than Harvard."

Something under half the general staff are full-time army officers, whose principal function is teaching, in basic-training schools and refresher courses. To learn what they are to teach, some of them are sent to the Swiss Federal Institute of Technology, in Zurich, and they also go abroad. They study at the German general-staff college, in Hamburg. They study at the École Supérieure de Guerre, in Paris, and the Royal College of Defence Studies, in London. They can be found regularly in United States Army schools at Fort Benning, Fort Leavenworth, and Fort Knox. Thoroughgoing professionals, they can be numbered in the low hundreds. In the Swiss Army as a whole, there are fifty thousand officers who are neither professionals nor members of the general staff, and what is most remarkable about them is—businessmen, bankers—how professional they appear coming out from behind their desks. It is impossible to say that the face becomes the mask, or the mask becomes the face, because the colonel and the barrister, the banker and the captain, the major and the businessman are one. In their uniforms, there might be a faint whiff of mothballs, but not in their military presence. Spread through the country with their troops, they suggest such establishment of command that they seem to be alumni of a West Point, of which Switzerland has no counterpart more exact than its banks.

Observed in their cadres, wearing their gold stripes and tailored green, as, say, they dine together in regimental headquarters at the Hotel Rhone, in Salgesch, they are—from Day One of a repetition course—very evidently cohesive, hierarchical, serious, and believably military, no matter where they may have been the day before. There is an atmosphere of shared experience. Companionable, familiar, they seem to belong together, and, from nuance to nuance, to speak their common language uncommonly in common. As one captain has delicately phrased it for me, "we don't want to have an upper-class officers' corps, but on the other hand it is not easy for a plumber or a mason to be with the officers." They are somewhat St. Paul's. That is, they are essentially old school, and in fundament ecclesiastic. Chaplains pray with them in the morning and bring them benediction at night. They break their croissants at six-thirty sharp. Beforehand, the young chaplain of the day may have brought greetings from his uncle, a retired colonel, and then used phrases like "No problem" while comparing life to a crossword puzzle wherein the vertical is love of God, the horizontal is love of man, and the two together form the cross. Seated at a long table and flanking Colonel Chaudet, they appear to be convened for the Last Breakfast. More than half of them have—or are working on—advanced degrees. Colonel Chaudet is said to be working on a possible candidacy for a place on the Federal Council, whose seven ministers are collectively the supreme national executive. His father, Paul Chaudet, was Minister of Defense some time ago, and twice took his turn as President of Switzerland. The Colonel is cool, a little shy, somewhat distant. Often, one hears said of him, "C'est le fils de son père." In their bright, evening moods, the officers sometimes call to mind stage scenes of old Heidelberg, as if the river nearby were, for the moment, the Neckar instead of the Rhone. Not a great deal of time has gone by since the days of the student fighting societies, which were as prevalent in Switzerland as in Germany—the Alt Helvetia Society, the Tigurinia Society, the Jurassia and Germania Societies—wherein the young future officers in the universities went at each other with one-metre swords. It was a tradition. They did not fight to "win," they fought to develop fearlessness and other forms of courage.

When I learned that Dr. Max Taeschler, a friend of mine in Basel, had belonged in his youth to such a society, I asked him, "Did you cut each other?"

He said, "Only in the head."

In Salgesch, over raclette and Fendant, I remarked one evening to the captain on my right that the atmosphere among the assembled officers suggested an English or American gentlemen's club. "That is an excellent definition of the army," he said. "That is it—exactly."

The major on my left commented frankly that he had put a great deal of effort into his military career, in part for patriotism and in part for the rank, because of its advantage in the civilian world.

The captain concluded, "If you are going to have a close tie between the citizenry and the army, you have to have an effect on the society, including the closing of some doors to non-army people. That, of course, is criticized."

In days largely gone by, to be a sergeant was more important in a village than to be a priest or the mayor. To become an officer was—in one's family—a matter of triumph or tradition. Not to be accepted for military service was a family shame. These durable criteria have diminished but have not disappeared. To be turned down by the army is a financial liability if not a complete shame. Doors close in the commercial world.

There are those also who do not accept service—two or three hundred young men each year who for religious and conscientious reasons refuse to serve—and doors are closed to them in the most emphatic way: they are tried in court and sent to jail. Sentences range from four to six months. Swiss Mennonites who refused to carry arms emigrated long ago to places like Iowa and Pennsylvania. Only on the ground of mental or physical unfitness can a Swiss male citizen be legally excused from the army, unless he happens to be a policeman or hold some other deferment job. The list is short. In 1977, a hundred thousand Swiss signed a petition that put on the ballot an initiative calling for alternative ways to do national service—hospital work or whatever. Eight to five, the people voted it down. The Federal Council has recently decreed that a soldier with his colonel's permission may serve without a gun. There is now a petition in circulation that calls for an initiative to abolish the army altogether. An initiative to abolish chocolate would stand an equal chance.

There are remarkably few graffiti in Switzerland. The most distinguished is Lord Byron's name, by his own hand, in the dungeon that held the prisoner of Chillon. The most intense are the terse initials that equate the Helvetian Confederation with the Third Reich: "CH = SS." A surprising number are in English: "STONED AGAIN," "KILL THE PIGS NOW," "THE SHIP'S A-GOIN' DOWN." Most of all, one sees the circled "A" of the anarchist youth movement that has ruffled the complacency of the republic with protest in recent years but seems for the moment to have subsided, to have acquired a complacency of its own. The circled "A"s increase in number with proximity to Zurich, proximity to Basel, proximity to Geneva. Generally speaking, the acceptance and esteem that the army enjoys among contemporary youth in Switzerland are in direct proportion to distance from cities.

"Can we count on the young generation? Yes. Yes. Yes. Be careful on this question. As commander of a regiment, I have found that young people in the seventeen weeks' basic training might cause trouble for one or two weeks only. After that, their psychological problems are negligible, and more or less don't exist."

"Basel, Geneva, and Zurich are not representative of Switzerland. There are critical, negative youngsters in cities. Youngsters are completely different in the Mittelland farm country and certainly in the mountains. If there are troubles, they are in the big towns."

"The army is an educational matter in Switzerland —not only a question of defense. Every Swiss age twenty needs to be shouted at a little and to have a good time with friends. He becomes a citizen who has a gun at home."

Young athletes, whose years of maximum ability are so elusively brief, have been known to appear at the army health examination with their bloodstreams full of alcohol, so their hearts would flutter like caged birds. Some are adept at simulating deafness in one ear. Not many are rejected outright. La Commission de Recrutement assigns them instead to the Service Complémentaire, to do a hundred days' duty over ten years— clerklike, without weapons. One Swiss athlete who quite undeceptively ended up in the Service Complémentaire was Jean-François Pahud, a first-rank distance runner twenty years ago. He was known throughout the nation as Le Long Pahud—a reference to his remarkable physique. Towering above the doctor in the examination room, Pahud, who could run five kilometres in fourteen and a half minutes, was told that he was unfit for the army because his chest was too small. To qualify for the Swiss Army, a man's chest circumference had to be half his height, and Pahud's was far from it. He was told to do certain exercises and return in a year. A year later, age twenty, Pahud returned. His chest had become even smaller. "Like all Swiss youth, I saw the army as a test of manhood," he recalls. "I hoped to be an officer. Only later did other athletes point out to me how lucky I was."

In the Service Complémentaire, he found the other athletes: the Swiss record holder in the shot put, the European record holder at two hundred metres.

Albert Einstein, who became a Swiss citizen at the age of twenty-one, was also rejected by the regular army. He had varicose veins and flat feet, and was assigned, like Le Long Pahud, to the Service Complémentaire.

Women may join the Service Complémentaire. For them, it is voluntary, but once they sign up they serve for fifteen years. They drive vehicles. They operate telephone and radio systems. They cook. They tend homing pigeons. I have heard all that referred to as "housewife work." Switzerland in 1981 passed a law assuring equality of rights to women and men—an equivalent of the Equal Rights Amendment, and a large step for a nation that only ten years before gave women the right to vote in national elections. In Appenzell, women still cannot vote in cantonal elections. There are no women on the general staff.

Jean-François Pahud is now the curator of the Olympic Museum, in Lausanne. A tall man with a great wash of silver-edged black hair, a prominent nose, a large black mustache, he remains more slender than a finishing nail. In the event of a national emergency, he says, every athlete would be on hand to do something about it.

Does he feel there is a need for an army in Switzerland?

He replies, "C'est clair."

With other parts of the battalion, Massy and the Section de Renseignements reported at noon to the garage in Brig where the bureaucracy of the Poste-Téléphone-Télégraphe regionally services its numerous buses, all of which were out on the road. The room was as big as an armory. The soldiers lined up to be issued sleeping bags, mountain jackets, rain capes, gaiters, Finnish hats, and surgical bandages. Thus their refresher course began, and they sat on their packs and waited. Lieutenant Wyssa waited. Captain Dessemontet. Massy, at the center of a cluster of soldiers, removed from his pack a bottle of wine. Massy's pack looked like a launcher of ground-to-air missiles. He began his refresher course with his tire-bouchon, raising the cork. He ran it past his nose, and unbuttoned his breast pocket, reaching for his little glass. "The purpose of the Section de Renseignements is to eliminate uncertainty," he said, addressing no one in particular, expect-

ing nothing in return—erupting with mock instructions
and aping the tone of an officer, as he often does, apparently to enjoy the sound as it raps the air. Following his
ritual, he filled the glass, wished good health to the soldiers around him, and drank. Then he filled it again, for
Pascal Layaz, twenty-two years old, a graphic artist
from Vevey, who wears a gold ring in one ear; for Pierre
Pillard, twenty-seven years old, a redheaded, red-bearded
fitter of false teeth, who works in Yverdon; for Christian Tanniger, Michel Frei, Bernard Parisod, house-
painters, of Lausanne, Vevey, Montreux; for Jean-Bruno
Wettstein, of Nyon. Reporting to Brig, in Valais, they
were all from the Canton de Vaud. Regiments still belong to the cantons, which have not transferred to the
federal government nearly as much right or power as
have the states of the United States. A person who earns,
say, twenty thousand francs a year in the Canton de
Vaud owes taxes of less than a hundred francs to the
confederation and eighteen hundred to the canton. A
person who earns a hundred thousand francs pays six
thousand to the confederation and twenty-three thousand to the canton. If a canton needs troops, it can take
two battalions from any of its regiments without re-
questing them of the confederation. In Lausanne, the
capital of Vaud, a green bronze statue dominates the
plaza between the Château Saint-Maire and the house
of the Grand Council. It is a likeness of Charles Veillon
(1809–69), described on the plinth as "Colonel of the
Army of Vaud."

In the bus garage, the proud soldiers seemed pleased
to be seeing one another—as who would not be, through
the bottom of Massy's glass? There was more to being

in the army than being in the army: they were back together. Sometimes in the civilian year, they have their small reunions. As an adjutant began shouting orders, each order was mimicked by someone obscure in the crowd. Massy smiled and poured the wine. Generally speaking, it can be said that discipline is nearly perfect in the Swiss Army, and that discipline is perhaps a little less than perfect if the soldiers are thinking in French, and, finally, that within any French-speaking battalion perfection tends to dilapidate in the Section de Renseignements. According to majors and manuals, Renseignements is an activity that calls for a special style of mind, constantly seeking intelligence and finding it even if it is not there, for in peacetime exercises what is required above all else is imagination. The effect of the Section de Renseignements is, in one major's words, "to make it live." The patrols of Renseignements walk in the unoccupied territory between the battalion and the enemy. They circle high behind enemy lines. Since the mountains are real and the enemy is not, there tends to be a certain diminution of energy during a refresher course—particularly on the part of those who go out on patrol, in contrast to those who stay in the command post and think up things for the patrols to do. Essentially, the people in the command posts are editors, trying to make sense of the information presented by the patrols, and by and large the patrols are collections of miscellaneous freelancing loners, who lack enthusiasm for the military enterprise, have various levels of antipathy to figures of authority, and, in a phrase employed by themselves and their officers alike, are "the black sheep of the army."

Of the five companies in each battalion, it is the Headquarters Company that includes the Section de Renseignements. Soldiers in the Section de Renseignements are drawn from each of the four other companies. More often than not, the captains choose from their companies soldiers they want to get rid of.

"Massy, did they want to get rid of you?"

"But yes."

"But why?"

"I have spent many days in le trou."

Le trou—known formally as the local d'arrêts and the arrestlokal—is where soldiers are locked up after they come in late at night, for example, or fail to clean their rifles, or drink themselves to paralysis, or go to sleep on watch, or shoot at téléphérique cables and high-tension wires. It is where many people thought a number of soldiers should have been put after they shot at center-fold photographs from *Playboy*. A captain can give three days in le trou, a major ten, a colonel fifteen. The soldier is locked up with a Bible.

"He has a window now."

"Because of the human rights."

When bullets hit high-tension wires, the wires flash with flame. When the soldiers used *Playboy* pictures as assault-rifle targets, the story was reported in newspapers and feminists burst into flame. The army said the fusiliers had shown bad taste. Various amici curiae asked why the women had let themselves be photographed in the first place—a question lacking an answer that would satisfy a Swiss.

Massy yanked at a pétard on a lieutenant's chest and got ten days in le trou. There was more to the story, of course, than just that. A pétard is a small imitation grenade—basically a firecracker. Like a grenade, it has a fuse, and it explodes six and a half seconds after the fuse is activated. The playful Massy intended to remove the pétard, fuse and all, from the lieutenant's chest, but the lieutenant slapped at Massy's hand and Massy succeeded only in activating the fuse. Six, five, four . . . There were fifty pétards on the lieutenant's chest. After the first one exploded, others sequentially exploded, too. The lieutenant became a walking sparkler. As Massy describes him, "he was running around like Donald Duck." Attempting to stop the chain reaction, the lieutenant took off his steel helmet and clasped it to his chest. There was great thunder and a burst of lightning as all the remaining pétards exploded together. Massy was paler than a white grape. He thought the lieutenant was "finished." The lieutenant, as it happened, was completely uninjured, needed only a new uniform—and it was Massy who, for the nonce, was finished.

Pillard—the denture technician—reacted against all authority throughout his seventeen weeks of basic training and thereafter found a home in Renseignements. Later, at Trient, on the road to Chamonix, Pillard refused to obey a corporal who wanted him to do some extra work, and he spent ten days in le trou.

Jean-Bruno Wettstein, as a result of his first repetition course, was among the select who were invited to seek promotion. He went to a doctor instead. He said he had no desire to command anything and did not believe in the army. He said he could not accept the phenomenon of war, believing it to be "absurd and stupid." The doctor told him that if he was not careful he would be coded psycho in federal files and the label would hamper him for the rest of his life. The doctor wrote a letter that emphasized both Wettstein's sanity and the extreme difficulty he seemed to have in accepting authority. Wettstein was excused from the army for two years. He went to Gascony and worked with goats. "We were going to change the world," Wettstein said of himself and others. "But the world did not change, and we did." Eventually, when he rejoined the battalion, he was, in his words, "almost automatically put into Renseignements."

The soldiers were dressed now in their gaiters, their mountain jackets, their Finnish hats. Packs on their backs, rifles across their chests, they left the P.T.T. garage and walked half a mile through the quiet streets of Brig. They were on their way to La Prise du Drapeau, a ceremony in which the battalion would bring forth from storage its hallowed flag, to be carried into putative battle.

"It symbolizes our fighting spirit," someone remarked.

And Wettstein said, "Fighting spirit is very important in football games."

Wettstein, once a long-distance runner, continues to be in fine condition through his work in the alpages. With amiable brown eyes and a ready smile, he softens the bite of his words. Straight brown hair lightly touches his shoulders. He is the son of a radiologist, and he grew up in Geneva, a city that, in his words, is full of "bad Swiss." One year, as an exchange student, he went to Linn-Mar High School, in Marion, Iowa, where he won his "L-M" in track. "The Republic and Canton of Geneva has been in the confederation only since 1815," he said, explaining his remark about his home town. "It is an international city with no strong Swiss traditions." Genevans sometimes say that it is not necessary to be stupid to be a colonel but it helps.

Passing German street signs and German shop signs, the soldiers walked through town to hear a speech in French.

"Who will speak?"

"The major."

"What will he say?"

"He will say, 'The purpose of the army is to keep Switzerland free. The Russians are not very far away. Have a good three weeks. Dismissed.' "

The soldiers left their packs in a small meadow and formed ranks on a green beside a school. In various directions, there was little to see but light industry, a church steeple, small apartment buildings, sheep, cattle, and fruit trees—until you looked up. Everywhere above were Alps—gold, red, and green on the lower slopes, white beyond the timberline: Glishorn, Hübschhorn, Klenenhorn, the framing peaks of Simplon; Riederhorn, Hohstock, Sparrhorn, ascending the Bernese Oberland. Clouds were streaming up the mountainsides, running through the conifers like smoke. All five companies of the Eighth Battalion were assembled at parade rest and waiting. The Divisionnaire arrived, and the regimental colonel, Chaudet—the Divisionnaire in a white Mercedes, the Colonel in his gray one. Lesser officers lined up flanking Tschumy and Chaudet, including Captain François Rumpf, of the Bankverein; Major Peter Keller, of Hoffmann–La Roche; Colonel Louis Gilliéron, of La

Suisse Assurances; and Major Jean-Daniel Favre, of the Schweizerische Industrie Gesellschaft.

The five companies stood and silently waited. The Divisionnaire, the Colonel, and the lesser officers waited. The Alps waited. Time came and went forever while they waited for the band. It is a tradition among Swiss Army musicians that Swiss Army musicians are unique and special and deserve to be treated as such, in a class by themselves, above schedules and—like nothing else in Switzerland—beyond the clock.

Captain Rumpf whispered, "They are prima donnas."

Thirty minutes after the Divisionnaire had appeared, the band showed up, wearing old steel combat helmets of the sort that faced west across the Western Front. They puffed with effort on their tubas and bassoons, and—unlike the waiting soldiers—could in no sense be described as élite. They were middle-aged, for the most part, with beards of assorted lengths and paunches as prominent as drums. They appeared to have come out of an American Legion hall on the edge of River City. They might have been holding their thirty-fifth reunion. With emotion, elegance, stateliness, they played the national anthem.

The flag was carried forth, and Major Jacques-Henri Beausire stood in a jeep and addressed his battalion. "Officiers, sous-officiers, soldats . . ."

Major Beausire, an independent economic entrepreneur, is a former banker, whose brush-cut hair and firm heavy build more readily suggested an emeritus fullback.

"Ce matin, vous avez déjà accompli un des moments difficiles. . . ."

The speech was inconvenienced by a Toyota fork-lift in a marble yard next door.

". . . laisser les siens pour une période de trois semaines . . ."

The machine sporadically burped, and only fragments of the speech came through.

". . . quitter son activité professionelle malgré les soucis de la période économique que nous traversons. . . ."

Seven tons of rock fell off the fork.

"Je sais que vous aurez à cœur de démontrer que les gens de votre âge ne correspondent pas forcément à l'image de la minorité qui nous est abondamment rapportée et décrite par les moyens d'information. . . ."

As the soldiers left the ceremony, Wettstein parroted the Major, saying, " 'You are here now and have made a great sacrifice to leave your homes and jobs. You are representing the nation and not a discontented minority of youth. . . .' It is the same speech always," he said. "It is the same speech as in the States."

Massy said, "It is written by the same person."

When I have not been out walking and collecting information with the Section de Renseignements, I have been in the charge of Captain Rumpf, whose "Little Book of Service" shows eleven hundred days. The latter ones may have been trying for him. It is possible that Rumpf would prefer to be crawling under machine-gun bullets. After I made application to the government in Bern—and was softwared, dossiered, and cleared—I received letters informing me that I would "serve" with units of the Tenth Mountain Division and be under the general surveillance of Captain François Rumpf. He is an adjutant of Divisionnaire Tschumy, and has completed two or three months of special training to become a major, which is not quite enough; as a final requirement he has been given the task of overseeing me. I alone stand between Rumpf and the broad gold stripe of a major.

Rumpf is forty-one. He married Juliette Roussy, a

daughter of the Dean of the Cathedral of Lausanne, and has three young daughters. When I first met him, in Basel, he was wearing a Cardin blazer, a yellow V-necked cashmere pullover, a white-collared blue-and-white-striped shirt, and an English club tie. My own daughters would call him megaprep. With his apple cheeks and boyish manner, he did seem like a teacher at Uppingham or Kent, but he proved to be in charge of all private customers, worldwide, for the Schweizer-ischer Bankverein. He appreciatively acknowledges that he was given the job because of his rank in the army. The son of two doctors, he grew up in Vevey. His surname notwithstanding, he is resolutely Suisse romand—pure Vaudois and so much so that he regards Geneva as "absolutely not a Swiss town," and goes on to remark, "You will see a lot of Arabs there." In one of those moments of amazed recognition when someone exclaims "It's a small world!" Rumpf genteelly disagrees. "I say it is not a small world," says Rumpf. "I say the upper class is thin." He served the Bankverein for eight years in Monaco, and is now posted to Basel, from which he sends his children—Sophie, Joelle, Laetitia—daily into France to school. His ancestors lived in Basel, but he says the people of Basel today would never understand his Bentley (which he keeps in France). They might regard as rather odd his passion for distinguished cars.

The army has given him and me a sick Opel. We get around, seeing people and exercises. We go into the hanging valleys. Rumpf is an aesthetician. He likes sunsets, snow-covered couloirs, vines in fruit, and Switzerland. He points out the lovely, rock-enlofted church in Raron—where Rainer Maria Rilke is buried by the south-facing wall—and on the road to Simplon he ignores the hidden cannons. He tends to treat the army itself as if it were a military secret.

We went into the Val d'Anniviers. The dendritic valleys of Valais, branches of the Rhone system—Blinnental, Lötschental, Mattertal, Val de Bagnes, Val d'Hérens, Val d'Anniviers—are so competitively beautiful that (as with most awards) no one valley can reasonably be chosen above all others. Having said that, if I could go into only one I would without hesitation go into the Val d'Anniviers. Up out of the Rhone Valley we climbed the switchbacks from Sierre. We were discussing events that might occur in a time of national emergency, and I was asking Captain Rumpf how the army might respond if an enemy were to insist that Switzerland surrender or be showered with atomic bombs.

"We will absolutely never give up," he said. "Ninety-five per cent of Switzerland is sheltered, and we are on our way to a hundred per cent."

We were passing through the village of Niouc. Already, we were twelve hundred feet above the Rhone, and the mountainsides close around us went up six thousand more. Moving on along the keelson of the Val d'Anniviers, we could see ahead of us some of the high Pennines—Grand Cornier, Dent Blanche, Ober-Gabelhorn. "Do not bring a tank into this valley," Rumpf counselled me. "You would be blown to pieces."

The deeply cutting river was called La Navisence. Villages, spread in the sun on their alpages, were two thousand feet above the river. Other villages—Saint-Luc, Saint-Jean—were on lower ground, the chalets dark and plain. In Grimentz, there was a waterwheel and dark granaries standing on flat round stones, and notices on the walls: "AVIS DE TIR." The people are the first to know when bullets will be flying. About fifteen kilometres from the Rhone, we moved close among the buildings of a town called Mission, where Rumpf parked beside a public hall. It had been a school—one large room on an upper floor—and for the moment it was the brain center of the regiment's Seventh Battalion.

"I'll just look in a moment and see if anyone's here," said Rumpf.

Major Jean-Philippe Jaussi was there, and Captain Ernst Sturzenegger, finishing, with other officers, their midday meal. "Come and join us," said Jaussi. "There is plenty." The old schoolroom was touchingly spare— a heavy-plank unfinished floor, a long refectory table— with a spread of windows, mountain light, and absent paper snowflakes. The food, presented with a dated menu, was remarkably unspare—a flavorsome light potage, choux-rouge braisés, fresh saucisson and jambon fumé, pommes natures, Poire Belle-Hélène—and in the glassware was a vigorous Dôle of the Valais. Captain Sturzenegger—a youthful man with a quick-forming grin—said in the course of conversation that in his civilian job with Crédit Suisse he was in charge of all the bank's personnel outside Switzerland: the nation's modern mercenaries.

Rumpf said, "You see the influence of banking on the army."

And someone said, "Not to mention the influence of the army on banking."

I remarked that Ernst Sturzenegger was a name

roughly twice as German as François Rumpf, and I wondered how Sturzenegger had come to serve in a Suisse-romand battalion.

Indeed, he was from Zurich, he said, and nothing about him was French but his colleagues in the army. In officer school, he had been told to translate something into French and had done so with ease. He was also sent out on a long walk, which he did not complete. Rubbing the one fact against the other, his superiors were pleased to reward him with exile, assigning him to a French battalion. In this way, the army deals with a chronic shortage: In French Switzerland, there are not enough officers to go around, not enough people who are willing to pay the grade, so the army must fill in with Swiss Germans. He said he had once been part of a Tenth Division company in which every officer was a Suisse allemand. There was contentment in his face and a playful smile as he completed this discussion. He said, "The French Swiss Army drinks wine, the German Swiss Army almost never." And he finished his chocolate pear.

Major Jaussi said the pear was for officers only. He called it "a little amelioration." The dinner had otherwise been served in various places to soldiers as well. I learned somewhat later that it had been prepared by a chef tournant from the brigade de cuisine of the Hotel zum Storchen, in Zurich. His name was Fredi Eckert—a tall, dark-haired twenty-seven-year-old cook with eyes as dark brown as finishing chocolate. Until quite recently, he had been cooking at the Hyatt Regency in Chicago. He had returned to Switzerland for the army some weeks beforehand, so that he could take up his new position at the Storchen and be paid his salary while off with the troops in the mountains. This was completely acceptable to the Storchen, whose general manager, Major Jean-Philippe Jaussi, would be in the same mountains at the same time, and in the same battalion, of which he is commanding officer. Jaussi had long known Corporal Eckert in the army, had employed him earlier at the Hotel zum Storchen, and had arranged his experiences in kitchens from Ticino to Vaud, in Nice, in Zurich, in Chicago. Jaussi regards his dual association with the chef as "typical of the importance of the army in civilian life." As chef tournant at the Storchen, Eckert had been working one day as saucier, the next as pâtissier, the next as garde-manger, and so on, amply proving to one and all that the hotel was fortunate to have him—not to mention the battalion, where his presence was more than a little amelioration. In this refresher course, in the battalion kitchen in the Val d'Anniviers, he had working under him as assistant cooks a biologist, an engineer, a baker, and a ship's officer from a boat on Lake Geneva. "I have always to look around," Eckert told me when I met him. "Sometimes they don't know how to take the knife in the hand."

Soldiers in refresher courses will typically eat in village restaurants, where they buy drinks but are served food that is carried into the restaurants by the army. Few battalions have a chef tournant as caporal de cuisine. On a table—serve yourself—there might be an army-colored ice chest full of lukewarm macaroni. A peck of oiled lettuce in a big aluminum pot. Some bread. Some cheese. No pears under chocolate sauce. The army kitchen staffs carry hot food wherever the soldiers happen to be. Rumpf and I were watching machine-gun practice one day, far up in the Saastal, several miles from the nearest road, in a thick snowstorm. The visibility could not have been more than three hundred feet. Around the white mountainside appeared a line of ice-bearded porters—looking for all the world like hired Sherpas—carrying brown ice chests full of hot carrots, rice, and stew.

Major Jaussi said that he was waiting for the sound of a helicopter. His mortar company was about to be inspected by the Commandant de Corps. The mortars had been set up a few miles away, and we would go there to meet the chopper. He spoke with enthusiasm about the usefulness of mortars. "For me, as battalion commander, they are my little artillery. They are precise. They are mobile, not too heavy. They cover three and a half to four kilometres. In the mountains, that is good. You can shoot from one valley to the other."

Thirty years ago, this same battalion—the Seventh Battalion of the Fifth Regiment of the Tenth Mountain Division—was commanded by Major Jaussi's father, Major Jaussi. If the present Major Jaussi were to win an international prize, I doubt that he would regard the fact with more affection. "In certain families," he said, "being in the Mountain Corps is a very strong tradition." In days that followed, I would come to know him, to talk with him at greater length than in the old schoolhouse in Mission, and he told me that when his father was not serving in the army he was being trained at the Meurice, in Paris, the Dorchester, in London, for the family has traditions in the hotel business, too, in both French and German Switzerland, reaching back through six generations. In 1969, Jean-Philippe Jaussi went to Cornell, for a semester at the school of hotel management, and in Ithaca, America, he found a truly novel world. "People said, 'Pop in. Pop in.' Wherever I went in America, people would say, 'Pop in. Pop in.' This American expression changed my approach to life. In Switzerland, it is impossible. Unimaginable. No one says, 'Pop in.' Or anything like it. My family had a big house in the country between Vevey and Montreux, about a mile back from the lake. If we wished to have visitors, my mother was always asking a week's notice. She would clean all the windows. Everything had to be perfect— the Swiss way. It's a little heavy. The Swiss are too well educated, a little too stiff, while the American says, 'Just pop in. You know where the fridge is. Just help yourself.' "

"Not this American," I murmured, zipping up my army cardigan against a mountain draft.

"If you speak French in German Switzerland, it is hard to get along, hard to make friends," Jaussi said. "Ithaca was a friendly, open world. At Cornell, they think Swiss are Swedes. Cornell never heard of Switzerland."

Jaussi had worked at the Waldorf-Astoria—and the Greenbrier, in White Sulphur Springs, West Virginia. "The Waldorf was a world in itself, a little city with people walking through the lobby, going from Park to Lex. It was like a bee house. In Switzerland, after midnight, there is not much going on. New York never ends. It is on a twenty-four-hour basis. I went everywhere—to Broadway, to the ballet, the Village Vanguard, Harlem. I was squeezing the lemon. I lived on

Eighty-first between Lex and Third. The Greenbrier, like the Peninsula Hotel, in Hong Kong, was run by a Swiss Mafia. Hermann Rusch, the Swiss chef, was there. Virtually all the key positions were Swiss. It was a resort lost in the middle of nowhere, with a village living on the hotel. A truck went to New York for goods twice a week. I worked under Rusch as garde-manger, among ice carvings and butter sculptures. I met Sam Snead."

Returning to Switzerland, he had applied for a job at the Hotel Zurich, and had made clear to his prospective employers his lifelong dual ambition: to manage a first-class hotel and to take the time as well to try to become an army major, to "match the achievement" of his father. He had every reason to suspect that his plan would be regarded with favor, because the Hotel Zurich —like the Hotel zum Storchen—was owned by Oerlikon-Bührle, a diversified company that manufactures (among other things) anti-aircraft guns, armored personnel carriers, and missile launchers, and has as its chief executive officer Colonel Dieter Bührle, a member of the general staff. Hired to do sales and marketing, Jaussi went off to Milwaukee, to Albany, to Kansas City, successfully drumming up trade. He was surprised when the Hotel zum Storchen job was offered to him, because, as a Suisse romand, he felt himself a bit of a foreigner in La Suisse Allemande. To run the hotel by the river in the old city—where Paracelsus had been a guest, as had Richard Wagner—he thought the company would want a Zuricher, with Zurich dialect, when all he could speak was High German. He was chosen because he was a captain in the army. It was simply "a matter of leadership." The Storchen has a cloistered arcade, a boat landing, and leaded windows that are extremely clean. It has a dining balcony over the Limmat. The diners wear dark-blue suits. Half are from Zurich and half from Philadelphia. They speak discounted Esperanto.

"We can provide the capability."

"We are willing to share the profit."

"We all can look forward to an adequate share of the market."

The Rathaus is across the water, and the Grossmünster.

Among the desk-drawer materials in the room of each guest is a document entitled "Jog with the G.M."

Dear Guest,
From Monday to Friday, you may join the General Manager of the Hotel zum Storchen for 30 minutes of jogging along the Lake of Zurich.
Please register with the Night Concierge . . . and you will be picked up at 6:15 A.M. sharp.

The sound of pounded air was coming up the valley. A few days before, Major Jaussi, in his three-piece pinstripes, protruding handkerchief, had been briskly patrolling the Hotel zum Storchen, a handsome and neatly groomed man behind gold-and-tortoiseshell eyeglasses, with dark straight hair, brown eyes—direct, earnest, open, engaging. And now, in much the same manner, with a wide gold stripe on each shoulder, he had his battalion in spread-out units all over the Val d'Anniviers, and he was in charge of what everyone was doing—at least until the helicopter landed. He had driven up the valley to greet the Commandant de Corps. This was a short, graying man who spoke slowly.

He explored for words. He had a kindly face that was somewhat wrinkled and drawn. There were three stars on his cap, and down the sides of his legs ran the broad black stripes of the general staff, disappearing into low black boots. Sometimes described as "mysterious," and "not well known outside Ticino," he was one of the seven supreme commanders of the Swiss Army: Enrico Franchini, leader of all divisions of the Mountain Corps. Ticino is the largely transalpine Italian-speaking canton, where the supply of army officers is even less abundant than it is in La Suisse Romande. Franchini is a luminous exception.

Under tamaracks near the headwaters of the Navisence, the mortar company had set its weapons. Dug in, levelled, they were aiming vaguely south. An order was given that they be turned around and reset in less than ten minutes—to deal with enemy units discovered to the north. Shovels churned. Base plates went down on the rocky ground. There was a great deal of tossed dirt and examining of imprisoned bubbles. The job done, Franchini looked things over. Franchini had served in a mortar company during the Second World War. He now went from crew to crew, mortar to mortar, base plate to base plate, and found all of them faulty. In the stony soil, the plates were not firm enough to please him. As he moved from group to group, he quietly lectured. Accuracy depended on the stability of the plates.

Standing apart, Major Jaussi said to me, "The mortar is a dangerous weapon if they don't know where they shoot. They shoot over the troops. If you are in the troop under the fire, you must trust them. We do such exercises, and they have to work."

"Before they shoot, what do they do to make sure it's safe?" I asked.

Captain Rumpf said, "They go to church."

Franchini polled the mortar crews, asking what they did "in life." They were cheesemakers, boat builders, masons, farmers. In shifting the mortars around, they had turned away from a short high view of the snowy Dent Blanche and other Pennine summits to a distant picture of the Bernese Oberland framed in the steep green valley, with its chalets and meadows, its snow-fields and forest. Franchini had not come for the view. He had singled out a corporal for particular instruction, informing him that his retreating manner and lack of bearing were at least as disturbing as his ignorance of mortars.

The corporal was nervous. He said, "Oui, mon Divisionnaire."

Franchini said, "Je suis le Commandant de Corps." Speaking further about the need for firm base plates, he asked, as he finished, "Compris?"

The corporal said, "Compris, Divisionnaire."

Franchini said, "Je suis le Commandant de Corps." He mentioned to the corporal that he would be a more effective leader if he stood up straight. Did the corporal agree?

"Oui, oui, Divisionnaire."

"Commandant de Corps!"

Franchini tended to gesture with his hands. Like a maestro, he moved them up and down. In one famous moment, when he was in a similar discussion with a rattled soldier, the soldier misinterpreted the gestures, reached out, and warmly shook Franchini's hand. This corporal, however, kept his arms at his sides, and did not seem to be thinking that he had made a new friend.

"A day without adequate preparation is a day lost," Franchini was saying. Did the corporal understand?

The corporal said, "Compris, Divisionnaire."

Gently, the Commandant said, "Je suis le Commandant de Corps."

"Compris," said the corporal.

If the corporal did not know what he was doing, he could not possibly lead others. Was that understood?

"Compris."

If he did not suggest in his own bearing a sense of purpose and pride, all discipline would disintegrate beneath him. Was that understood?

"Compris. Compris."

If the base plate were to shift in the ground, the shell could end up in the battalion's headquarters. Was that clear enough?

"Compris. Compris."

Service compris.

"Fermez les bouteilles!" barked Massy, in his voice of mock command. After the flag ceremony, he and his company were served stew in the meadow where they had left their packs, and now it was time to move—to climb about a thousand feet to their quarters, in Ried, a village said by Lieutenant Wyssa to be a ninety-minute walk from Brig. Massy was by no means the only soldier who had brought wine for the noonday meal, but he alone had brought a glass. The others drank from their bottles. A hundred and thirty speckled gray packs were lined up in neat rows, like granite tombstones, near the joking, reuniting soldiers, whose automatic rifles were resting on their bipods by the packs. A soldier with an apple in his hand was sleeping on the ground. For a time, he went on sleeping while the rest of the company stirred.

Before long, Lieutenant Wyssa gave an order a good deal more official than "Fermez les bouteilles." The Section de Renseignements, moving out past the marble yard and the remorseless Toyota forklift, ambled in a southerly direction through the fringes of the town. As before, they did not march; they walked—single file or double or triple, at the soldiers' choice. "Serrez! Serrez!" Wyssa called out, trying to keep them together, for they tended to be vague, like strollers on an evening paseo instead of a typical Swiss infantry unit demonstrating its precision and anticipatory responses to command. "Serrez! Serrez!"

Even within the limits of Brig, there were Brown Swiss cows and black-nosed Valais sheep. There were stone barns. I asked the agronomist Jean-Bruno Wettstein if—as in the high alpages—the little barns were called écuries.

"In the French part of Switzerland, we don't speak French very well," he said. "Actually, an écurie is for horses, and an étable is for cows. The Swiss mix the terms. They use them interchangeably. If a place has room for animals and people, it is called a chalet d'alpage."

We moved under a road sign that said "SIMPLON ITALIA," and soon left the road to walk beside a stream. It was called the Saltina, and it came from the mountains around Simplon Pass. Rushing white, it was having a last word before expiring into the Rhone. The soldier walking in front of me could not hear the noisy water. He had earphones in his ears, and the wires ran inside his mountain jacket. "In the Section de Renseignements, we try to decide what is the intention of the enemy," Lieutenant Wyssa said to me, in a voice pitched high to ride over the sound of the stream. "We seek information, and sometimes it seeks us. Before we can use it, we must decide if it is true, probable, or false." I asked him what he had studied at Penn, and he said, "Anti-trust and tax law."

Leaving the Saltina, the soldiers climbed a short, steep trail through woods and reached a road that doubled back to a high stone bridge across the stream. It was called Napoleon's Bridge, and Napoleon was said to have crossed it with an army at some point on the road to Elba. The soldiers were quoting Napoleon: "Les meilleures troupes, celles auxquelles vous pouvez faire le plus confiance, ce sont les Suisses!" A Valais mercenary battalion worked for Napoleon in Spain and Russia.

"The French people are not rid of him yet," said Jean-Bruno Wettstein.

The bridge spanned a gorge that no terrestrial vehicle could cross on its own. Small steel doors in one pier hinted that Napoleonsbrücke was ready to blow. It had been superseded, however, by an even higher bridge, which leaped through the sky above—a part of the new road to Simplon. In an extreme emergency, the midspan of the new bridge would no doubt drop on the old one.

Set back on the flaring lip of the gorge was a spread of numbered squares: 1, 2, 3, 4, 5, 6—a three-hundred-metre target range. One sees such ranges near every village and town: against rock outcrops, across meadows as smooth and green as cricket pitches, halfway up hillsides backstopped with forest. Shooting rifles is a national sport. It is also compulsory. The national shooting contests—the Knabenschiessen, the Wyberschiessen, the Rütlischiessen—are major annual events, even more important than the Steinstossen, in which the object is to heave as far as possible a rock that weighs a hundred and eighty-four pounds. (The Swiss—and therefore world—record is three and a half metres.) Meanwhile, soldiers in all age groups practice at their local shooting ranges and must demonstrate adequate competence once a year. Massy goes to the range up the hill behind Epesses; Wettstein goes down the road from Nyon to targets set up close to the French frontier. In their annual test, they fire twenty-four shots, some rapidly, some at will, against plain and camouflaged targets. There is a point system, with a perfect score of a hundred and twelve. If they fail to score fifty-two, they have to put on their uniforms and report to Lausanne for two days of shooting under instructive supervision.

Wettstein said, "I score in the sixties. I'm not a very good shooter, even if I try. Once, I did well. I had a ninety-one."

"You closed your eyes and had a lucky day."

"No. My brother went for me."

"Serrez! Serrez!"

One of Wettstein's childhood heroes was the runner Jean-François Pahud. When Wettstein spent his year at Linn-Mar High School, in Marion, Iowa, he was a middle- and long-distance running star. So impressed are the Swiss with the accomplishments of Swiss in the United States that the entire top floor of the Musée des Suisses à l'Étranger, outside Geneva, is given over to the subject. There is a lovingly framed photograph of the basketball team of Berne High School, in Indiana. There are snapshots, newspaper pages, and so forth from Switzerland County, Indiana; Tell City, Indiana; New

Bern, North Carolina; East Bernstadt, Kentucky; New Glarus, Wisconsin. There are testimonials to the families from Ticino who emigrated to Asti, California, and made Italian Swiss Colony wine.

An oil portrait of General Johann August Sutter, of Basel, presents him with a broad-brimmed flat-topped hat above crafty blue eyes and a gray handlebar mustache—looking much like, and even less military than, Harland Sanders, of Kentucky, the chicken colonel. Sutter, of course, was a general nowhere, least of all in Switzerland—but he founded New Helvetia, California, whose name became Sacramento after gold was discovered there, in 1848.

Portraits and paraphernalia of the most major figures march down the walls of the museum's attic rooms.

Albert Gallatin, of Geneva, instructor in French at Harvard, United States representative, United States senator, Secretary of the Treasury at the time of the Louisiana Purchase.

Louis Agassiz, of Neuchâtel, one of the most celebrated professors Harvard has ever had, who convinced the world of the validity of his theory that ice two miles thick had once spread widely over Europe and North America.

William Wyler, of Oberehrendingen, in the Canton d'Argovie, director of "Wuthering Heights," director of "Friendly Persuasion," director of "The Big Country," director of "Ben Hur."

Louis Chevrolet, of La Chaux-de-Fonds, Canton de Neuchâtel, who emigrated to the United States at the age of twenty-one, undertook to make motor vehicles, and placed on the front end of each of them the enduring emblem that "n'est pas sans rappeler, de façon stylisée, le pays d'origine du constructeur"—that is, the map of Switzerland.

Othmar-Hermann Ammann, of Schaffhausen, civil engineer, variously designer or builder of the Golden Gate Bridge, the Verrazano-Narrows Bridge, the Hell Gate Bridge, the Queensboro Bridge, the Triborough Bridge, the Throgs Neck Bridge, the Bronx-Whitestone Bridge, the Goethals Bridge, the Bayonne Bridge, the George Washington Bridge, the Lincoln Tunnel.

So proud is Switzerland of its progeny in America that mention is made even of Solomon Guggenheim, who was born in Philadelphia to parents born in Switzerland.

"Serrez! Serrez!"

The stragglers coalesced beyond Napoleon's Bridge.

Soon we were looking far down on Brig from high rural ground, a breeze in our faces, the Saltina delta and the Rhone Valley deep in the lee of the Bernese Oberland. Turning the other way, we faced the Hübschhorn, all white and half in sunlight up the pass. Wettstein said that while the Simplon Tunnel was being built, before the First World War, the army attacked striking workers. In 1932, when there were political riots in Geneva, the army killed thirteen civilians and wounded eighty. "The army defends against the enemy and preserves internal peace." He also said that the public rampage of recent times by discontented youth had become "minor, small scale," and was "not representative of Switzerland; young Swiss today have become conservative and less absorbed with politics, as they have in the States."

We went by small farms with block-lettered messages on the farmhouse walls beseeching God to guard them. We passed cherry trees that were now as orange as maples. There were more black-nosed sheep, and, at every turn, the universal cattle, with the tintinnabulation of their bells, bells, bells—the clink and clank and clangor of the bells.

A chalet under construction irritated Wettstein. "These are hay meadows," he said. "And there is a problem if they are used for construction. In the mountains, there is plenty of room for grazing but not enough for hay." Since the Second World War, in a steady attrition, Switzerland has lost to development nearly forty per cent of its productive agricultural land. When Wettstein was ten years old, he decided he wanted to be a farmer; but in Switzerland—as an expression goes—it is more difficult to become a farmer than to become President of the Confederation. A farm of, say, sixty acres would cost more than a million dollars if it were available, and that is unlikely. Wettstein settled for agronomy. To the south of us, beyond the Hübschhorn, he had worked not long before at a chalet d'alpage that sends milk plunging by pipeline three kilometres to the village of Simplon, where it is made into cheese—assuming it is not butter when it arrives. Describing the operation, Wettstein quoted J. Robert Oppenheimer on the development of the fission bomb, saying it was one per cent genius and ninety-nine per cent hard work. Wettstein has also put in some months trying to improve the deteriorating chalets and bad grass of Bourg-Saint-Pierre, near the Grand-Saint-Bernard Pass. At Vernamiège, high up the side of the Val d'Hérens, he cleaned up the overgrowth on abandoned agricultural terraces—restoring the land, removing the fire danger, and kicking out the vipers.

"The . . . ?"

"Snakes. They are poisonous adders. They are all over Switzerland. They are not good for tourists. There are many in Valais—everywhere up to two thousand metres."

"What is our present altitude?"

"Eight hundred metres. They don't bite much. You have to step on them. No one is killed by them. They are mostly dangerous to children."

We walked by small perfect squares of standing corn, tan now and dry, stiff as hairbrushes among the grazed meadows. We walked by huge cabbages. Wettstein said, "Children in Switzerland are born in cabbages, so the cabbages must be large."

And eighty-nine minutes after the climb to Ried began, the Section de Renseignements arrived in the center of the village. "Eighty-nine minutes," said Massy. "Lieutenant Wyssa told us ninety. He doesn't lie too much."

It was a village of small homes and a few granaries standing on posts interrupted by broad discs of rock, keeping rodents away from the grain—a simple mountain town no larger than Epesses, and not nearly as compact and ornate. Incongruous in its center was a dark-wood-and-concrete modern school. It sat on a foundation so generously poured that the building seemed to be about two-thirds basement. A large L-shaped entryway led into the basement. A sentry with rifle stood at the bend in the L. Most of the soldiers waited outside—waited to be issued more clothing, extra gear. A swarm of farmers in uniform—who are known as soldats du train because they deal with horses—were singing and swilling in groups. One after another, the Vaudois soldiers went up to the village bulletin board and squinted at a language they could not read. "They discover the geography of Switzerland," said Corporal Philip Müheim, who works in an import-export office in Vevey. "This army is more human than military. We are militarily ten or fifteen years behind, but the army is a tradition." The Swiss school system tends to separate people from the age of twelve according to background, intelligence, and future profession. In the vital way that the American public high school draws together the skeins of American society, the Swiss Army knits Switzerland.

Wettstein said, "If an enemy comes, the whole thing will be over blitzkrieg fast."

Dark was coming on, and the air was cold. When at last it was time to go inside, Massy and the others carried their gear past the sentry in the doorway and went in under the school. The basement door, standing open, was nearly two feet thick and was made of concrete framed with steel. Its hinges were like cannon barrels. Inside were rooms enough—room after room after room—to contain the population of the town. Latrine, showers, kitchen—all of it was under a concrete ceiling three feet thick. It was not the fate of the Section de Renseignements to sleep in a room near the door—to have whatever advantage such propinquity might provide. They had been assigned to a room beyond a room—blank-walled, with sixteen double bunks filling up most of the space, foam mattresses on the bunks. Massy climbed to an upper bunk and sat there looking depressed, with his legs dangling. In bunks around and below him were Pillard, Wettstein, Tanniger, Layaz, Schyrr, Pera. After unrolling a towel, Massy slowly elevated the cork in a bottle of Clos du Boux Epesses. He looked dismally around the gray walls of the village bomb shelter. His glance was arrested by a long galvanized tube suspended like stovepipe from the ceiling and designed to bring in fresh air. Lugubriously, he said, "La fenêtre."

There was a two-centilitre pause between "la" and "fenêtre." Massy poured a taste of wine. To come into the army, he had left his cave, and now he was back in a cave. Soldiers unpacked, stretched out, dealt cards. Massy passed the glass to the right, and jumped down from his bunk. He had noticed in the rear wall a small steel door secured with large levers, like a hatch in a submarine. He lifted the levers and, with considerable effort, swung the door open. It was about three feet by two, and nine inches thick, and weighed at least six hundred pounds. On the other side was empty darkness. Without so much as putting on a yellow slicker, Massy entered this cuve of cuves. Not for nothing was he in Renseignements. He vanished into the darkness. There were sounds of upward scuffle. Soon he came back down. His head appeared in the hatchway. "Trees! I saw living trees!" he said. "It is the emergency escape. There is a way out of here. We can leave after lights!"

During the Second World War, as the Swiss observed the destruction of cities around them, they had no difficulty imagining such scenes transposed to Switzerland. They were particularly alarmed by the firestorms that killed large percentages of the civilian populations of places like Hamburg and Dresden, and they set out to learn what they could about how to prevent a similar devastation of Zurich. After the war, they sought out as a consultant a former Nazi major general who had commanded fourteen thousand soldiers fighting fires in Berlin. They learned, among other things, that the civilians of the German cities had roasted to death in basements that were swept over by fires moving from one to another of the lightly constructed buildings above—deaths that might not have occurred within walls and ceilings made of thick concrete.

In the late nineteen-forties, Swiss people building private homes and apartment houses voluntarily used such construction. In the fifties came subsidies and regulation—the forty-centimetre concrete ceiling—but still the official purpose was to protect the population from destruction such as had occurred in Europe during the Second World War. Not until twenty years after Hiroshima did Switzerland shift its attention to the Third World War and begin to design shelters against the effects of nuclear weapons. The Swiss in the nineteen-sixties had no idea what such a program would cost, nor did they attempt to work out a cost-benefit ratio, because they saw the benefit as both imperative and infinite, and therefore inexpressible in arithmetical terms. The author Jonathan Schell, writing in a different and wider context, recently expressed the Swiss point of view exactly when he said, "A society that systematically shuts its eyes to an urgent peril to its physical survival and fails to take any steps to save itself cannot be called psychologically well."

After studying Samuel Glasstone on "The Effects of Nuclear Weapons," and all related unclassified material, the Swiss eventually settled on the concept of the one-bar shelter. A bar is a unit of pressure—of the sort that explosions make—and is equivalent to ten metric tons per square metre. Walls and ceilings can be built to withstand such pressure. Close to a nuclear explosion, pressures are of course much higher, and in that zone people in one-bar shelters would be lost, but as the pressure wave spreads, it declines rapidly. At Hiroshima, a one-bar shelter might have saved lives half a mile from the bomb. At Nagasaki, too. The pressure wave from a hundred-kiloton bomb (five times the size of Nagasaki's) would decline to one bar in somewhat under a mile. One megaton—two and six-tenths kilometres. Two megatons —four kilometres. Five megatons—five and a half kilometres. Twenty megatons—eight kilometres. Very few warheads are as large as that.

Conceding general destruction on the closer ground —and assuming bombs exploding anywhere—the Swiss started building one-bar shelters to protect the extremely high percentage of the population that might survive explosions but without shelter would be destroyed like the citizens of Hamburg and Dresden. Swiss calculations showed that something as thick as, say, a ten-bar shelter would be of negligible extra value, for the increased area of protection would be slight rather than proportional; for underground hospitals and command posts, three-bar construction was chosen. Light and heat from a nuclear explosion that would blind and severely burn a person who happened to be outdoors would at the same distance have no effect on a person in a one-bar shelter. Arriving with and soon after the light would be gamma rays and neutrons—radiation against which the shelters must include adequate shielding. Water is adequate, and there is a good deal of it in concrete. Early fallout, downwind, occurs through twenty-four hours—and arrives in pieces as large as coins, ranging on down to dust. If the pieces are sucked in by shelter ventilators, they are stopped by filters.

Particles emitting radiation also cling to dust that hovers at high altitudes or travels around the planet and when it falls cannot penetrate a one-bar shelter. Civil-defense experts of various countries agree that two weeks in the shelter will cover the worst possibilities of delayed fallout. But—as a civil-defense engineer once explained to me in Bern—"even when radiation is down, it is still high by peacetime standards; you do not go out and walk with the children." His name was Friedrich Sager, and he was vice-director of Swiss civil defense, in charge of all household shelters, including the large ones, such as Massy's military bedroom. "One hour after the explosion, you go out and measure the intensity of the radiation," Sager went on. "If it is very high, you go back in. After two days, it will have decreased a hundred times. An explosion in a nearby country could be a serious fallout problem. Neutrality helps not at all. After one or two days, you can go upstairs—assuming there is an upstairs —take a bath, feed the pet. If you have previously closed all doors and windows, you will have minimum particles in the house and none in the shelter. So this gives you an opportunity to make a warm meal, take care of the little doggy—it's only a matter of time, O.K.?—and then get back into the shelter. You stay in the shelter as long as you can. Three weeks, if you can. In a good shelter, you can say, 'My home is my castle.' "

Water is more important than food, he pointed out. And, like air, water that is exposed to radiation does not become radioactive and can be filtered. On this matter, out of curiosity as much as anything else, Swiss civil-defense officials asked their English counterparts how much water Lord Nelson carried on his warships. The answer was less than four litres per day per man. In all shelters, from private ones in houses to big ones sleeping whole towns, people are supposed to supply their own food. "First, they bring their fat," Sager said. "They can live on that for at least a week. The average household keeps food enough on hand. There are no requirements for stocking shelters." Anyone who has built a house in recent decades has, by force of law, a shelter at home, usually full of ski boots and wine. All over Switzerland, one sees schools and public buildings resting like the tips of icebergs on their enormous one-bar basements. All over Switzerland, in relatively spacious and quiet towns, are sophisticated underground parking garages with automatic machines that offer tickets like tongues and imply a level of commerce that is somewhere else. In a nuclear emergency, huge doors would slide closed with the town's population inside. In the charming old sections of cities, with their astigmatic windows, and timbers that creak like wooden ships, no effort has been made to add shelters under the buildings. Big public shelters have been developed instead. There is a garage in Zurich that is ready for seven thousand people. The biggest bomb shelter in the world is the Sonnenberg Tunnel, in which an Autobahn traverses Lucerne. In a nuclear emergency, doors high enough and wide enough for the hangar of a rigid airship would slide on rails and close the tunnel. Made of tessellated slabs of concrete, the doors are five feet thick. There is a command post inside, and a hospital, and sleeping accommodations for twenty thousand people. Environmentalists are at present attempting to prevent the construction of an Autobahn tunnel through the Bernese Oberland. A friend in Basel once said to me, "If environmentalists had been around a hundred years ago, there would now be no place to hide."

"The principal remaining problem is to shelter small clustered rural communities, but farmers will never build shelters," Sager told me. "They are thinking in litres of milk. The only solution is higher subsidies. Epesses? You never touch such a village with shelters. It is too beautiful. Instead, put a big hole in the ground. Persuade the people to keep their wine there. Epesses today has almost no shelters. In peacetime, they could use one not only for storage but for drinking and eating, too. They could enjoy themselves. How is it they call such a cellar? Ah—a carnotzet."

To be informed about radiation levels, direction of fallout, and the progress of war, any shelter large or small wants to be in close communication with a command post. Civil-defense command posts are meant to cover about twenty thousand people. Sager took me into one below a firehouse near Bern—a three-bar shelter fourteen feet deep, with outer walls twenty inches thick. We went down a narrow flight of stairs into an airlock, then into a room with two showers, and then into a dozen more rooms, glistening clean, with many rows of telephones, electronic equipment, telecommunications equipment, triple-deck bunks, a stocked kitchen, a diesel generator, and twenty-four hundred litres of diesel fuel—all in place, ready. In the conference-and-recreation room, a large mural had been painted by visiting schoolchildren—a primitive in primary colors—of cable cars and boats, castles and balloons, Swiss cities and country, Swiss mountains and the moon. There was a blackboard on which someone had written these words exactly: "McKill-Roy Is Watching You."

Such a deep token of preparedness implies a deeper history of threat. From the joining of the first three cantons to the army maneuvers of the present day, Switzerland has existed to repel offensive neighbors, and with regard to this subject has never felt complacent or relaxed. It would be very un-Swiss to wake up tomorrow to yesterday's threat and then attempt to do something about it. If Pearl Harbor had somehow been in Switzerland, a great deal of Japanese aluminum would be scattered all over the Alps. Never in modern times, of course, has threat to Switzerland been more continuous than from 1939 to 1945, and while underground command posts with walls as thick as Dunsinane's may have been designed in the nineteen-seventies according to the science of nuclear-weapons effects, they are also hidden monuments to the anxieties of the Second World War.

While actual battles were being fought to the west, the north, the south, the east, simulated battles were taking place inside Switzerland. To keep itself prepared, and abreast of new technologies, the Swiss Army imitated the war that was going on around it. During the siege of Stalingrad, during the desert campaign, during the invasion of Sicily and the Battle of the Bulge, Swiss soldiers in Switzerland were firing weapons identical or equivalent to the weapons then in use in the war. They were fording rivers in full battle dress, stringing barbed wire, bivouacking in deep winter snows, scrubbing their laundry in summer streams, climbing rock faces with machine-gun parts, hauling cannons into high alpages. They were always on patrol—on skis, on foot, on motorcycles, on bicycles, in boats.

Now and then, they shot down a trespassing aircraft. Other planes, damaged, requested and received permission to land. Some, abandoned by pilots and crews, just drifted into Switzerland and crashed. An empty American B-17 hit a medieval castle and filled its tall tower with flaming gasoline. A Red Cross library on international peace had been put in the tower so that it would not be damaged in the war. Imagining themselves to be over Germany, twenty American bombers dropped four hundred bombs on Schaffhausen, Switzerland's northernmost city. A German plane carrying an experimental package of supersecret radar made an unintentional landing near Zurich, possibly guided by the supersecret radar. The Swiss seized the radar and hid it in an alp. The Nazis threatened invasion. The Swiss offered a deal. They brought the radar out of the alp and destroyed it in the presence of German witnesses in return for a dozen fighter planes, on which the iron crosses were repainted white.

Early in the war, as the rest of Europe blacked out,

Switzerland still sparkled with light and served as a beacon to aircraft of any description. The Germans were particularly uncomfortable with this flashlight at their side. They told Switzerland to shut off the light or Germans would come and do it for them. Switzerland went dark. Switzerland had mobilized when Germany invaded Poland. The Swiss imagined that their turn was coming, too. In months that followed, as fear of invasion temporarily declined, many men were sent home "on leave" —each with his gun and forty-eight bullets—only to be called back when Germany invaded France, Luxembourg, Belgium, and Holland. Motion pictures were stopped in mid-performance. Announcements were read. Swiss soldiers were ordered straight out of the cinemas and into the field. Mobilization, always rapid, expanded with each successive threat and declined soon afterward. Whenever things looked bad, more than four hundred thousand Swiss soldiers were at their battle stations. Things looked bad when Germany piled up beside the Bodensee enough munitions, matériel, and implied manpower to relocate Switzerland in Sardinia. At times like these, there was some panic. A significant piece of the population of Basel departed. At least two thousand never came back. Cars streamed across the country with mattresses on their roofs to absorb possible bullets from the air. The pile of matériel by the Bodensee turned out to be a ruse to divert attention from an attack in preparation elsewhere. In 1940, the Germans and the Italians actually did form a plan to attack Switzerland. The Germans meant to take Geneva from France and then cross the Mittelland to Bern. They would also come down past Basel to Lucerne. Meanwhile, the Italian

Army was assigned to capture the Alps. The German code name for all this was Tannenbaum. The plan included a map of the Axis apportionment of Swiss territory. The Germans were to get the Mittelland, the Italians the rocks.

The Swiss knew nothing of Tannenbaum. But they imagined something like it. Paintings and stained-glass windows went into storage underground. From time to time, attack was not just feared but anticipated. When German armies entered Denmark and Norway, the Swiss expected them to come south as well. After France was gone, rationing became general, and eventually included such things as pet food and flour and (perhaps worst of all) chocolate, but by neighboring standards the rationing was not severe: the people were denied meat two days a week. Also after France surrendered, the German military attaché sought out Jakob Huber, the Swiss chief of the general staff, and made it clear that he felt the time had come for Switzerland to open its doors and welcome a German Europe. There was a six-decilitre pause. Huber studied the attaché and said, "No one comes through here."

Some things did go through here, however—in sealed trains. People wondered what was inside. When coal trains went through, no one could see what was under the coal. By the terms of a 1909 treaty, the coal itself was permissible, as were wheat, oil, timber, steel— all of which went through Switzerland on the way from Germany to Italy. The trains came back with vegetables. For Switzerland to permit war matériel to pass through Switzerland would have been an abdication of neutrality: no less a deception than if Henri Guisan were to

dress as a civilian and ride a train out of Switzerland to
strengthen his connections with the French—as he did,
not long before the outbreak of war. Switzerland played
both sides for the middle. For the Allies, the Swiss
manufactured ball bearings, jewel bearings, theodolites,
chronographs, machine tools. In 1941, under German
pressure, the Swiss government decreed that packages
could not be sent abroad, thus cutting off shipments of
small precision parts to Britain. For the Axis, the Swiss
made fuses, timed as fine as clocks. They made ball
bearings for the Nazis, too. In June of 1943, the British
dropped a few bombs into an industrial section of Zurich
—a message in exploding code. When the Swiss Army
learned of German plans to assassinate General Dwight
Eisenhower and General Jean de Lattre de Tassigny,
they described the plans to the Americans and the
French.

As Switzerland was subjected to various threats and
pressures, particularly from the north, it was the art of
General Guisan to bend just enough to avoid fracture,
to grant an hour to gain a day, to sell a little something
but not to sell out. He was a Vaudois farmer—a Suisse
romand who openly detested the Nazis of Germany,
and he was in charge of a nation in which a dismaying
minority did not share that view. While his military
task was to train his army and hold it ready to fight, his
political objective was to dissuade all the people who
were prepared to accept a German Europe, and his
social goal was to rally the Swiss, to quell their fear, to
replace their sense of helplessness with a sense of defensive strength—to keep the mattresses off the roofs of
the cars. Canton to canton, he travelled the country,

making his presence felt, urging soldiers and civilians to "Act Swiss! Think Swiss!" He said, "Switzerland can only avoid the threat of a direct German attack if the German high command, while preparing such an attack, becomes convinced that a war against us would be long and costly, that it would create a new battleground in the heart of Europe, in a most useless and dangerous way, and thus jeopardize the realization of its other plans." Accordingly, he advertised the preparedness of the army. He tried to toughen Switzerland internally while causing Switzerland to look tough from the outside. Given the will, the wherewithal, and the mountains, he said, the Swiss can keep anyone out. He made it absolutely clear to the Germans that if they invaded Switzerland the first thing they would hear would be a concerto of explosions as Switzerland's strategic railroads effectively ceased to exist. Highway bridges would be gone in the same moment. The knowledge of Switzerland's prepared demolition brought German saboteurs, who came to cut the wires, preceded by German spies. They had to be good to get to the wires or they found themselves in le trou. American, Russian, British spies—so many spies were in Switzerland during the war that they moved like slips of paper in a stock exchange. They were from every country but San Marino. Variously, they were spying on Switzerland, spying on one another, and using Switzerland as a telephone booth in which to report what they had been doing elsewhere. They met by matchlight under the dark arcades of Bern. Among them were Swiss. Fifteen Swiss traitors were executed during the war, most of whom were in the army. After they were sentenced, they were almost immediately killed by firing squads from their own army units.

Swiss schoolchildren are taught that Germany decided not to invade Switzerland because Germany knew that its losses would be too great—in what has become the classic phrase, "the price was too high."

"The Germans invaded the Dutch. The Dutch had declared themselves neutral. The Germans didn't come here, because of the Swiss Army."

"That's what I was taught in school. But then I have heard that it's not so simple."

"Did Switzerland avoid war as a result of the strategy of the great powers or the policy of neutrality or the strength of the army? We'll never know."

Near the end of the war, the Swiss went into mobilization one last time, because they foresaw a desperate Germany coming in to make defensive use of Swiss communications, and they also worried that the Allies might come through on their way to Germany. If these events had happened, the Swiss insist, they would have engaged in the war, fighting against both sides. In fact, Joseph Stalin did propose an Allied rampage through Switzerland, ostensibly en route to the evident enemy. Stalin hated the Swiss. He called them "swine." A month or two after his proposal, and perhaps by way of reply, Winston Churchill wrote to Anthony Eden: "I put this down for record. Of all the neutrals Switzerland has the greatest right to distinction. She has been the sole international force linking the hideously sundered nations and ourselves. What does it matter whether she has been able to give us the commercial advantages we desire or has given too many to the Germans, to keep herself alive? She has been a democratic state, standing for freedom in self-defence among her mountains, and in thought, in spite of race, largely on our side."

In August of 1945, in the square in front of the Ionic columns of the Curia Confoederationis Helveticae, in Bern, General Guisan stood before thousands of soldiers and civilians and received in formal ceremony their profound gratitude. The Swiss were celebrating the end of the war as if they had won it, and they had.

In late-evening darkness outside the bomb shelter in Ried, Captain Eric Dessemontet's Headquarters Company assembled in the town plaza and, in response to the captain's sharp commands, stood at something less than attention. There were those among them who swayed, leaned against one another, and occasionally broke into song. The plaza was essentially a wide spot in a small street. Automobiles kept arriving, and the soldiers had to break their ranks to let the cars go through. Called back into formation, they tended to huddle instead, noisily addressing one another while Dessemontet addressed them. "Taisez-vous!" he shouted, but they did not shut up. Between shouts, he said, sotto voce, to me, "I want you to know this is not unique. I always have this problem."

One might readily imagine that the problem was in the Section de Renseignements, but it was not. Within the assembled company, the Section de Renseignements stood quiet, at attention, and steady, like half a dozen rows of counted sheep. They may see themselves as headstrong, willful, insubordinate, but by comparison with the horse soldiers they are wimps to a man. Not only were the horse soldiers spackled out of their minds, they were also continuing to drink while they were meant to be standing at attention. They were farmers, for the most part—Vaudois farmers, from Rougemont and Château-d'Oex, towns en route from Montreux to Gstaad. For a farmer, going to the army can be less of a duty than a release, an only vacation, a celebration up the sides of the hills. An American colonel once told me, in careful words, that his impression of the Swiss Army was of "a different kind of discipline," of an order of magnitude "more relaxed than ours," but he added that in time of emergency such behavior would disappear. Even as the horse soldiers were flapping in formation like sheets in the wind, Massy remarked, "They are good, good people, the best we have."

The headlights of another automobile were slowly approaching through the standing ranks of soldiers. Some moved one way, some another to make a breach and let the car pass. The horse soldiers stayed put. They had been shouted at, cajoled, and told to stand still, and now they were not in a hurry to move for this car. From where I stood, the lights made silhouettes of them all— a black-on-gold unsteady tableau. Eventually, by ones and twos, they slowly moved aside, until only one soldier blocked the car—arms at his sides, chin tucked in, a body framed in headlights. One soldier, one automobile, one stalemate. Behind him, a booted foot lifted into the air, in silhouette moved slowly forward, and came to rest on the soldier's backside, centering on a spot eleven centimetres under the belt. The soldier was cata- pulted out of the scene, opening the way for the car.

Captain Rumpf and I went down one morning to see horses come off a train in Sierre. The army rents them from farmers. It is using three hundred in the present exercises, and this particular shipment was arriv- ing from Winterthur. An owner had been up all night with the horses, in the cold and lurching freight cars, and now—dressed en bleu de travail—he looked not only tired but also intimidated as he presented his ani- mals to Peter Keller. A doctor of veterinary medicine, Major Keller would decide if a horse was acceptable and—in case of accident—how much it was worth. Given his appearance, no one was likely to argue. Major Keller is a giant, an old-fashioned Swiss giant, in height, in frame, in voice, in beard, in motion—a giant. If he was not careful, he was going to knock over a freight car, and meanwhile he was looking down, with not unkindly eyes, upon this little wide-eyed farmer, who was scarcely five feet tall. The farmer led a horse down a ramp and, holding its halter, ran it up and down the cobblestone platform, his panting breath mixing with the steam from the nostrils of the horse.

"Thirty-two hundred," said Keller.

The owner looked relieved. Every horse, like every soldier, has its book of service, and this one's showed that it had first served the army three years ago. Its name was Barette. Others were Felix, Fauvette, Fleury, Flicka. They were big heavy draft horses reminiscent of the one beside the wall of Troy. As each horse gained Major Keller's approval, a soldier in knee-length boots and a ruddy camouflage jacket stepped up and led it away. The horse and the soldier would spend the entire refresher course together, going far up into the mountains beyond roads, up declivities beyond the grasp of four-wheel drive—the soldier walking, the horse in the traces of a two-wheeled pneumatic-tired cart full of rifles and personal gear and explosives, or food, or building materials, or bazookas, or ammunition, or hay. Officers ride. Soldiers walk. Among the soldiers was the usual preponderance of farmers, but there are not enough farmers anymore to match the number of horses, and also stepping forward to claim horses were a butcher, a mason, a painter of cars, a structural geologist, and an economist. The economist said he wished he could be in the cavalry, but this was all that was left. (He might have chosen bicycles. There are three bicycle regiments in the Swiss Army.) Horse and soldier would work and sleep in snowstorms. As a soldier led an animal away, sometimes both were hanging their heads.

"They walk and walk and walk," said Captain Rumpf. "The advantage is they don't need any petrol."

"Today, people laugh," said Major Keller. "Ultimately, we will have to go back to horses. Even now, when the weather is bad and the helicopters cannot fly, one is a hero to come into the mountains bringing supplies and hot food with horses."

There is no shortage of veterinarians in La Suisse Romande, but there is a shortage of veterinarians willing to give up the time to be officers, and since all army veterinarians must without exception be officers Major Keller has been borrowed from La Suisse Allemande. He works in toxicology for Hoffmann–La Roche, and may become a university professor. Only his habilitation stands in his way—a Germanic academic custom requiring as a condition of employment that a new professor have a completed and unpublished manuscript, by way of flooding instant credit upon the new employer. Albert Einstein, slow with his habilitation, worked in the patent office while waiting to teach at the University of Bern.

Peter Keller is a paradox of transportation. He deploys horses in the high Alps and in Montana rides Greyhound buses (stopping off to visit ranchers). In Switzerland, despite the national dimensions, he prefers most of all to fly. He is a pilot. On Sunday spins in rented Piper Archers, his routine is almost always the same—from Basel to the Bernese Oberland and across the Jungfraujoch divide, then over the Aletschgletscher and La Place de la Concorde Suisse, and then across the Rhone and up the Mattertal to circle the Matterhorn clockwise. Sometimes he lands in the Alps, in places so high, he says, "you need a good machine to get away with four people, otherwise they stick to the ground."

At the regimental headquarters one evening, Major Keller asked me if I had heard about the helicopter crash.

I said, "Yes. Last week in Grisons. What a shame. The pilot and the soldiers died."

He said, "Oh, no, not that one. I mean yesterday. Here in Wallis. It was another shame. There have been four accidents in the past week. Two jets. Two helicopters."

I said, "Peter, I am going to be spending a fair amount of time in helicopters, and right now I am eating my dinner."

He said, "They hit the wires. They always hit the wires. Sometimes farmers put up temporary wires and you cannot see them. Yesterday, again, the pilot and all the soldiers died. They had young children. They had children ten, twelve, fourteen years old."

At the Military Department in Bern, people were saying that there had actually been four and a half accidents. The half was a military policeman who fell off his motorcycle while escorting a foreign general.

Of one sort or another, there are a hundred thousand cables strung up the mountains of Switzerland. The country is a cat's cradle. One of the helicopter pilots was a forestry professor from Zurich flying five soldiers who were to play the role of enemy. Apparently blinded by the sun, the pilot hit a wire, and the helicopter fell into a gorge. The pilot had discussed that specific wire in the course of his preflight briefing. Meanwhile, a Swiss fighter pilot shot down another Swiss fighter pilot. The two were practicing. Making use of the Alps for military purposes in machines traveling near or beyond the speed of sound requires a great amount of practice— just to fly among the mountains, let alone to shoot.

"They can't miss one second. Otherwise, they run into a rock. They practice a lot. They also have a lot of accidents."

Airspace is so limited that some training is now done in Sweden, but there is only one place to practice flying in the Alps. The jet pilots fly low in the valleys and close to the rock. Nearly all Swissair pilots are in the Swiss Army's air force—and some doctors and dentists as well. They choose their own training time, and they need a good deal more than three weeks a year to learn to do what they can do. The air force is an example of contemporary technology demanding more time than a militia is set up to provide. Like specialists in electronic warfare, the pilots give extra time. When conditions are what they want for practicing, they take their Mirages, their Tigers, their Hunters and go. They develop incredible skill. They don't seem to use maps—having so little glancing time, having every contour in their heads. During the Second World War, after a Swiss pilot shot down a German bomber over the Canton de Neuchâtel the Germans sent fighters along on a mission that deliberately traversed Swiss air. Swiss pilots engaged the Luftwaffe in a dogfight and shot four Germans down. Victors and vanquished were using German airplanes. Swiss pilots now have infrared equipment and fly the mountain valleys at night. They can hide in the Alps. They know where they are and where to go. An enemy foolish enough to follow them will end up farming rock. At Gornergrat one day, at the top of a cog railway five thousand feet above Zermatt, I was sitting in an almost windless stillness, slowly moving my gaze in full circumference from the Breithorn to the Matterhorn to the Dent Blanche to the Zinalrothorn to the Weisshorn to the Dom—all well above four thousand metres—and on to the Dufourspitze, the highest mountain in Switzerland. Up out of the Mattertal came a Swiss Mirage. It skimmed over Gornergrat and dived toward the glaciers below. Its inclination appeared almost vertical, and it continued its dive until there seemed no chance that the plane could miss the ice and the pilot survive, but then it was climbing the glaciers close to the crevasses until it was deep in the cirques on the shoul-

ders of the Dufourspitze, over which it rolled to plunge
out of sight toward the Mattmarksee. The pilot was
probably taking pictures. Mirages work for Renseignements. The jets sometimes fire on targets and then, like
high jumpers, flip over ridges upside down. It is a way
to stay close to the rock. Their armament depends on
their mission. Variously, they carry cannons, missiles,
bombs. Even when cloud cover is extremely low during
exercise engagements with the enemy, if someone calls
for air support he will almost surely get it if there is any
kind of airspace between the cloud and the ground. The
Mirage drops out of the cloud, fires on the target, disappears upward in the cloud. It happens again a minute
later. The target is destroyed twice. The cloud is packed
like a snowfield among the Pennine Alps.

At Axalp, over the Brienzer See, the military attachés of at least twenty-five nations—including the
United States, China, and the Soviet Union—sat down
one day for a show. As the program began, a Mirage
appeared from nowhere, rattled the reviewing stand, did
a back flip over the Schwarzhorn, and was gone. Before
the program ended, each attaché was handed a photograph of himself looking up with startled expression.

We have inched our way down the valleyside and taken the Nussbaum bridge—that is, taken notes on its width, its tonnage, its lack of prepared demolition. Beneath it is the bouldery Rhone, with long clear pools, short riffles and chutes. Among the renseignements the battalion needs to know is the answer to the question "Can the river be crossed here on foot?"

Massy sketches on paper the river, the bridge, and the flanking mountains. He says, conclusively, "It is possible to cross the Rhone on foot, but there is no advantage."

Jean-Bruno Wettstein says, "Massy has a great sense of strategy."

Denis Schyrr goes off to collect statistics on the Bettmeralp téléphérique. The others lean over the bridge parapet and fly-cast with their eyes. Trout rise. To pass the time, I remove from my mountain jacket my copy

of "Armée Suisse." It is a paperback of small dimensions
with a water-resistant cover, designed for a soldier's
pocket. Words on the back say, "In the country of the
citizen-soldier, 'Armée Suisse' is an indispensable book.
It answers with precision all questions relative to the
national defense." In three hundred and seventy-two
pages of fine thin paper, it describes the organization,
strategies, and equipment of the army, discusses rights,
regulations, individual functions—all the basic facts a
soldier should know. It is a semi-official volume, which
is not given free to troops but is distributed through
bookstores everywhere in Switzerland.

Wettstein asks, "What is the book you are reading?"

I hand it to him. He looks it over with considerable
interest, having never seen one. The others crowd around
like students around a yearbook. None of them has seen
"Armée Suisse" before, although it has been in print for
several years and is revised annually to keep the Swiss
soldier up-to-date. On the back is a color photograph of
a fusilier walking on the edge of a glacier, carrying a
pack and wearing a steel helmet, his assault rifle suspended across his chest and his dagger hanging from his
hip. Wettstein says, "There you have the Swiss soldier
expressing his love of neutrality."

"Armée Suisse" has many photographs of Swiss
equipment—from the F-5E Tiger to four kinds of grenades to tanks, bicycles, howitzers, and guided missiles—
with accompanying statistics, such as weight and range
and explosive charge. Much of the Swiss Army's equipment is American. Some is British, some French. Switzerland buys tank ammunition from Israel. Russians are
distrustful of Swiss neutrality in part because Switzerland

buys nothing from them. The Swiss are militarily thrifty
—so much so that one would think at times that this is the
Scottish Army. While acquiring new wonders in infrared
vision, electronic deception, and computer warfare, they
continue to make use of equipment that is essentially
obsolete. Swiss pilots fly jets that are older than they are.
Until recently, Swiss paratroops jumped out of three
Junkers 52s, German transports from the Second World
War. The planes were wanted by museums all over
Europe, but they were not for sale. The army still uses
Centurion tanks that were made in Great Britain thirty
years ago. To keep such things in service is a tradition.
During the Second World War, there were Swiss artillery pieces on line and ready to fire which had been on
line and ready to fire since 1882. The Swiss throw nothing away, but their equipment is plenteous and for the
most part modern. They use McDonnell Douglas Dragon
rockets. Fifty years ago, when Swiss tank commanders
went out in the field for exercises they would say to
one another, "Shall we take three or all four?" Now
they have many tanks, if not as many as they think they
need. Most are state of the art and are made in Switzerland. The tanks do not yet have laser fire control, but
they will be acquiring it soon. The principal Swiss
artillery piece is a self-propelled howitzer made in the
United States. They call it "the American gun." To
increase the shooting distance, they have changed the
tube. Whether they design their own equipment or buy
it, they act with extreme care, always looking for sim-
plicity. They chose the F-5 over the F-16 because with
less difficulty they could keep it in the air.

The valley narrows where the river has cut a gorge.

La Place de la Concorde Suisse

At Grengiols, we cross a small bridge some two hundred feet above the water and follow a road chipped out of cliffs. Down the couloirs opposite, streams fall straight through forests under the skyline rock and on through green meadows to the Rhone. Farms are widely spread through the meadows. The rock above the tree line is largely covered with snow. The scene rises so steeply it seems painted on a curtain or a wall. From time to time, Haflingers, Pinzgauers, jeeps go by, providing glimpses of hats beribboned with gold. Officers ride. Soldiers walk. Up the road a few kilometres is Lax. The Major needs to know how large a military force could go past Lax without going through it. How much negotiable space is there in the level part of the valley? We will climb a thousand feet or so in order to form an opinion. The patrol will also choose a site for a new command post. Before attempting such a climb, they have thirst to be taken care of, and rest is called for, too. Close behind a small barn, in a meadow of purple dianthus, the patrol lies down. The barn is only a few metres wide but is an adequate screen from the Haflingers, Pinzgauers, and jeeps. It is written that no soldier out on patrol may go into a public building except on official business. So who will risk le trou to fetch some beer from Lax? Glances fly back and forth, cancelling one another out, until all eyes rest on the American observer.

A third of a mile from the barn, I find a market in the outskirts of town. I buy five litres of beer, and hold them like babies as I go back up the road. There is gratitude behind the barn, a certain something unspoken, too—a clear indication that, as General Guisan might put it, I have begun to think Swiss. I have earned my first cattle bell, and things look good for an oak-leaf cluster.

A boy happens by on a bicycle. Massy calls to him and offers him beer. Eagerly, he comes around the barn and drinks. He is seventeen, possibly. Most of his hair is dyed orange, and the remainder is Chinese red. As he drinks, an earring sways from one ear.

We climb now, away from the road, past a few houses and on into steep woods. Two small children come running out of a house and, following us, shout, "Bis . . . cuits! Bis . . . cuits! Bis . . . cuits!" By custom, kindly Swiss soldiers give cookies to kids. All we have to give them is beer. After a while, they abandon the chase, and their cries fade slowly behind us. "Bis . . . cuits! Bis . . . cuits!"

Lax is lovely from far above—a tall clock tower, an opulent ancient Valais town. Near a white church steeple, a lone maple blazes red-orange against a dark-green meadow. Renseignement: not much of an army could go past Lax without plowing through it. The valleysides are too abrupt. Far below us, among the chalets and barns, the cattle and meadows, we see rifles stacked outside tents, a dozen soldiers—no less expectable in a Swiss landscape than the ecclesiastical cows.

We descend obliquely through forest and pasture, cross the rails of the Furka-Oberalp, and continue up the Rhone. The light is falling as we go. It is dark when we reach the edge of Fiesch, with one more assignment to complete. There is a hydroelectric plant beside the river, but the water in the turbines is not from the Rhone. It comes from high in the Alps above, through a penstock drilled in the rock. The battalion needs to know the plant's capacity. It needs to know from exactly what place in the mountains the water descends. It needs to know if there are rungs or steps—some sort of cat-walk—in the penstock. But the hydroelectric plant is closed and dark. The air is cold now, and fanned by the fast-moving river. We are standing on a bridge leading to a locked door, and there is nothing to do but shiver.

Headlights turn toward us from the valley road. Miraculously, a Volkswagen Beetle descends to the power-plant bridge, crosses, parks; and a bearded man with a clipboard gets out and goes inside. Lights come on. The control room has tall plate-glass windows. We see him reading meters. Denis Schyrr and Pierre Pera follow him inside, but the engineer speaks no French and they speak no German. Of the five men in the patrol, only Jean-Bruno Wettstein speaks German. At the Swiss Federal Institute of Technology, in Zurich, he learned agronomy in German. Wettstein talks to the engineer. He learns that if a company of soldiers had to do it they could climb the mountain on the inside.

While Massy and the others are out on patrol, mortars pound the Mattertal, and the enemy is swept with pink tracers in the Val d'Anniviers. Soldiers with rifles and khaki rope belay down a cliff above Simplon Pass—hanging like spiders at the end of their silk. The Swiss forces are well spread out—each of the five companies in a battalion averaging, say, nine kilometres from the nearest of the four others, with the result that the army is less vulnerable to the enemy and more visible to everyone else. As any tourist can testify, the Swiss Army is probably the most visible army in the world. In every part of the upper Valais, soldiers are in action.

Each new day adds to the complexity of this multiple-exercise montage. Fusiliers begin to move in co-ordination with machine guns and, before long, with mortars—soldiers on their stomachs under other soldiers' bullets: machine-gun bullets shifting back and forth from one target to another while advancing fusiliers send bursts from their assault rifles; the two layers of fire conjoin.

The Swiss make the claim that they do things in exercises no other army would do. No one disputes the claim. The Swiss are the sort of people who like to shoot apples off one another's heads. Bullets fly close. Grenades explode close. Artillery and mortar shells drop nearby. Flamethrowers throw flames above crawling soldiers. When American troops in training crawl under machine-gun fire, the barrels of the guns are resting on metal supports below which they physically cannot move. Swiss machine guns are set up without constraints, exactly as in battle. A machine gunner has told me that he fired twenty-two thousand rounds in a single hour over the heads of other soldiers. He said the only accident he could remember happened when someone in his company fired a mortar over a mountain and into the next valley, where the shell exploded and killed a cow. In rounds fired—a military statistic of the first importance—the Swiss Army compares favorably with all other armies. Ammunition is expensive. Use of it begets skill in the use of it. Rounds fired is a classified matter everywhere, because analysts use the numbers to assess preparedness.

One afternoon, the military attachés went into the Canton de Fribourg to watch hundred-and-six-millimetre recoilless rifles being fired at targets across a public road. Automobiles were on the road. In case anyone should be wondering, it was explained that the drivers were travelling at their own risk, because notices had been posted—"AVIS DE TIR"—in the nearest communities to one side and the other. Machine gunners behind the attachés opened fire over their heads. "I was ready to hit the dirt," one of them said later. "I've been shot at before." A platoon of Swiss riflemen moved forward under the machine-gun fire. Another platoon, off to the right, was contributing rifle fire, too. As the first group moved ever farther forward, the riflemen to the right smoothly adjusted their fire so the bullets would not hit the advancing platoon. All these soldiers were essentially novices, in their fourth week of basic training.

Families sometimes visit units in training and watch them perform exercises. Several months ago, a blank mortar shell bounced off a wall and killed the fiancée of a soldier. Artillery shells, lost in high ground, have been fatal to hikers. Now and again, soldiers die in accidents in army vehicles, and not long ago a soldier fell off a rope bridge and drowned in a river. A woman in Geneva once told me that a friend of her family had lost three fingers to a grenade, and she added bitterly, "It seems so unnecessary when he's never going to have to fight a war."

Her husband lowered his fork. He said, "You hope he's never going to have to fight a war."

Under the Schwarzbergalp, above the Mattmarksee, machine guns, grenades, and rifles in concert open fire. The soldiers seem a little absurd, wearing brown-black-green-and-red camouflage capes in two feet of October snow. In winter, they wear white. The enemy approaches. They respond by throwing snowballs. It is a way of indicating to others where they mean to throw grenades. Now a smoke puff the shape and color of an eggplant comes up from a grenade—and another, and another—while echoes crash on the Schwarzbergalp and avalanches drop like veils.

Machine guns blaze in the Lengtal, four hundred metres above Lax. A helicopter touches down, carrying the Divisionnaire, a councillor of state of the Canton de Vaud, and other itinerant observers. The pilot is asked to move. He has landed on the target. He hops to safer ground—near a tall freestanding white cross, beside the church of the village of Heiligkreuz. Over the ridge, in the Rappetal, rifles, bazookas, and grenades are filling a ravine with smoke and splintered steel. The soldiers are tired, having climbed at night into this cold valley. Arriving before dawn, they slept a few hours on the ground —a student, a butcher, a gardener, an electrician, two farmers. Routinely, soldiers will walk all night in hard rain in order to reach the mountain setting from which they will attack. After arriving, they wash, shave. They prepare and eat hot food. They clean and oil their rifles. Still sleepless, they go into action—in logical formation, with eight to ten yards separating each man from the next. Unskilled soldiers will advance in bunches, congealed by herd instinct. Fire one shot at them and they all spread out—like the Swiss, who lack war experience but are well trained.

On a high slope of the Mattertal, three thousand feet above the valley floor, the noonday sun is shining, and the air is still and warm. Small barns, roofed with slabs of slate, go down to the river like stepping stones. From under a camouflage net, a carpenter fires a mortar vaguely toward the Matterhorn. The Matterhorn appears to be a railroad spike driven through the earth from the other side, or, with its canted summit, the beckoning finger of God. The helicopter ignores the Matterhorn, and, climbing a higher mountain, rises up the face of the Weisshorn. It climbs the rock a grain at a time. It hangs like a lamp before the wall of granite gneiss—Weisshorn: fourteen thousand seven hundred and eighty-two feet—and then floats across the summit ridge into the Val d'Anniviers.

Major Jaussi is there, at eight thousand feet, with his machine guns firing. The guns are shifting rapidly from target to target, firing their tracers into rock. "We have old machine guns," Jaussi remarks. "But in the mountains you need strong material. And these are very precise." They weigh seventeen kilograms. Their tripods weigh sixteen kilograms. Their ammunition (six hundred rounds for each gun) weighs twenty-seven kilograms. All this has been carried up here on the shoulders of the crews. The guns fire in three-second bursts—fifty bullets a burst. Major Jaussi inserts his words between bullets. "The enemy has been discovered," he says. "We want to make surprise fire. Therefore, the two machine guns must open fire together." Automatic rifles join in. Bullets rain into a north-facing cirque across a stream called the Torrent du Marais.

On even higher ground across the valley—the top of a five-hour climb—soldiers are advancing beside an avenue of machine-gun fire into a cirque that is rouged with alpenglow. In two feet of snow, eight soldiers, two with bazookas, cross a rise, fall prone, open fire.

An atomic bomb has exploded in Zweisimmen. The ubiquitous Major Jaussi is now in a village basement, in a house he is using for a command post, deep in the valley. He has received orders to move his battalion to

Château-d'Oex, using only mountain routes, for all movement by road is impossible. Overnight and into tomorrow, he and his captains and lieutenants have to figure out how to do it, and get the battalion started, and plan an attack from Gstaad. Captain Ernst Sturzenegger sits beside him. Words are sharp, formal, intensely serious. It is an exercise of the brain of the battalion. The battalion's A.B.C. man—atomic, biological, chemical expert—has already calculated the fallout and what routes to follow. "This is a test of the leaders in a stress situation, close to the real thing," Jaussi explains. Around the building are coils of barbed wire. There are wooden barricades. Airport-size searchlights, at eye level, periodically come on and sweep the night, sweep from house to house in the village. In the clips of the sentries' rifles, the bullets are no less real than they are in the mountains.

A hundred kilometres to the northeast, red helicopters have landed on the Rigi, bringing troops to join a battle in the valley below. On any given day, there is a battle almost anywhere, for "Switzerland does not have an army, Switzerland is an army," as the Swiss are wont to say. The enemy main force is coming down from Lake Constance and is using gas. The Rigi and the Rossberg are subalpine mountains that flank the Valley of Arth and Goldau, south of the Zuger See—in Schwyz, the forest canton for which the Confederation was named. Red tanks are moving south into the valley against established Swiss positions, while red infantry moves along the slopes of the two mountains to close in on the Swiss in pincer attack with the tanks.

The Swiss force is a Landwehr brigade—men in the thirty-three-to-forty-two age group, by dint of time no longer élite. Landwehr brigades are not mobile, like the

élite troops. Landwehr brigades do their refresher training in the place they would defend in war. The exact
territory of a Landwehr brigade is classified, but for
Infantry Battalion 188 it is more or less this valley. In a
deep fog, the soldiers are dug in and fighting. Many are
in foxholes, with fresh dirt piled beside them. Spread out
in ones and twos, they cannot see from foxhole to foxhole. Visibility is less than a hundred feet. The fog is
cut only by the throat-clearing sounds of automatic
rifles, of machine guns ripping like surgical tape. A man
in a gas mask is dug in beside a road in Oberarth. He is
under a camouflage net, and he wears a camouflage cape.
Intently, he watches the road, all but a bit of it obscure.
He has an assault rifle in his hands, and when the enemy
tanks come into view he will use it to fire anti-tank grenades. He has waited long, and no tanks have appeared.
A man on a bicycle emerges suddenly from the fog—a
civilian, middle-aged, with a pipe in his mouth. He rides
by, does not seem to notice the soldier, and disappears
quickly back into the fog. Across the road is an orchard,
and each tree—apple, cherry—is more distinct than the
one behind it, evanescing in the fog. Close behind the
foxhole, two cows appear, clinking. In their curiosity,
they extend their heads under the camouflage net and
on either side of the soldier. All three watch the road.

The fog suddenly lifts, all in a moment, as if a light
had been switched on in a room. There are sidewalks,
houses, apartment buildings, light industry, a school. A
Gulf gasoline station is just up the road. There are people on the sidewalks, people on bicycles, a woman behind
a baby carriage. The battle is waging not in some remote
alpine cirque but in the precincts of a populous town.

Now there is more rifle fire, machine-gun fire. No one
so much as looks up. Conversations on the sidewalks do
not even pause. The sound might as well be the sound of
rumbling trucks. In this community, battlefield noise is
just background noise—routine, possibly reassuring. Citizen army at work. Everyone knows the ammunition is
blank.

The fog has dropped again, as rapidly as it lifted.
The soldier in the gas mask is an electrician, and he wonders if I am legitimate. I am accompanied by Lieutenant
Siegward Strub, a friend from Basel, who arranged for
me to be here. The soldier turns upon him the flat-glass
stare of the gas mask. Strub's uniform notwithstanding,
the soldier seems to be wondering if Strub is a lieutenant.
The soldier demands identification. Strub gets out his
wallet, offers his papers, and makes a note to commend
the soldier. To see a Landwehr brigade—and, inciden-
tally, a German-speaking battalion—I have taken a day
off from the high mountains and journeyed into the fog.
The battle can be followed by ear—by listening to the
artillery and the mortars, by listening to the machine
guns and the rifles, and, most of all, by listening to Strub.
He grew up in Goldau, a mile up the road, and now, in
effect, has returned with the brigade to defend his home.
Walking through the orchard, we come upon machine-
gun nests equipped with anti-aircraft tripods—the better
to bring down helicopters. The fog is now so deep the
guns could not bring down an apple. The men—two in
a nest—are under camouflage nets and are wrapped in
camouflage capes as they lie beside their machine guns.
They look middle-aged, thin on top, well fed. They
have periscope binoculars and infrared sights. Some-

where out there in the fog, red infantry is creeping in, hoping to surprise them. The machine gunners, quietly talking, do not appear to be nervous.

"It's in the air," one of them says. "Something will happen soon."

"What is in the air?" says the other.

"Fog."

For the moment, cowbells in the orchard are the only sound. There is an occasional burst from an automatic rifle. The machine gunners have been in the nests most of the night and day. They take turns going off to a stable to sleep in sleeping bags on straw.

Moving on under the branches of plums, walnuts, and pears, Lieutenant Strub and I soon see in the mist the tall marching columns of the Autobahn to Saint Gotthard crossing a crease in the side of the Rigi. We can scarcely see the outline of the roadway. We hear only the wave-lap swish of the cars as they pass overhead. The road is a four-lane highway to the most strategic Swiss alpine pass, and so it is not surprising that in one of the support columns is a pair of metal doors. Strub looks questioningly at me, and I tell him I know what they are. He says that the miners (the demolitionists) are back in the fog somewhere: in houses, or out-of-doors under nets —in any case, well hidden, he has no idea where. He says the miners are the most secretive people in the army, and when he is having a beer with them and casually asks questions they have no answer for two out of three. For example, he has asked how many metres of this bridge would fall into the orchard if the reds were on their way to the pass. No answer. In their hideouts, meanwhile, the miners have nothing much to do, so they shuffle a deck and play Jass. It is a game with partners and trumps and what have you—a sort of bridge demolishers' bridge. Strub says, "It helps kill time efficiently." Who but the Swiss would have such a talent?

"We say in Switzerland, 'In every country, there is an army; here it is better to have our army than another one,'" Strub remarks, offering his endorsement of the military enterprise. He is a slender man in his thirties with bright brown eyes, a dark mustache, and thick prematurely gray hair that rises straight from his forehead before yielding to gravity and tumbling to the rear. His father was a railway engineer, operating the precision instruments that in other countries are known as trains. Sigi—as Lieutenant Strub is called—went to the University of Zurich and developed an interest in classical genetics. He found that virtually every important paper in the field had been written in English. Translations by and large did not exist. So he began reading English— novels, newspapers. For the better part of four years, he avoided his native German and every other language but English. When he presented his doctoral dissertation to the faculty in Zurich, the dissertation was in English. It was called "Developmental Potentials of Male Fore-Leg Imaginal Disks of Drosophila Melanogaster," and on the strength of it he won a postdoctoral fellowship at the University of California, Irvine. Later, he taught at the State University of New York at Stony Brook, Long Island. Now he is licensing manager for the pharmaceutical division of Sandoz, in Basel. He likens the Landwehr to a net, always in place. "I know exactly where, if the Russians come, I will fight. In this battalion are country people. With them, there is an x and a y axis and maybe a z axis, and that's it. If I had to face a war, I would like it to be with these people. If a lieutenant went ahead, they would follow. We come from this canton and are integrated into the general society here —more, sometimes, than we like, for the supply of schnapps is so constant. In Basel, we drink coffee with kirsch in it. Here we drink kirsch with coffee in it."

The fog is away again, and now we can see not only the Autobahn over the orchard but also the passenger trains on the side of the Rigi, going to or coming from Saint Gotthard. They slide by in comparative silence. They run on falling water. There is a tunnel. Soldiers are ready with bazookas, grenades, and automatic rifles to hit anything that happens to come through it. Machine guns and rifles are firing in the orchard. When machine guns erupt, the tempo of the cowbells does not increase. A woman with a small child drives among the trees in a station wagon. Bazookas are trained on the road, ready for the tanks. If little Haflingers appear, they are meant to be Schützenpanzers—eleven-and-a-half-ton tanks that can go sixty-five kilometres an hour carrying a twenty-millimetre cannon and seven grenadiers. If Pinzgauers appear, they are meant to be heavy tanks. If Fiats appear, they had best be ignored.

Again, the fog drops heavily. After Mark Twain was on the Rigi, in 1878, he wrote, "The fog lifted and showed us a well-worn path which led up a very steep rise to the left. We took it, and as soon as we had got far enough from the railway to render the finding it again an impossibility, the fog shut down on us once more." Fog favors the attacking side. The guns become relatively quiet—an occasional pop . . . pop . . . pop. While

Strub goes off to perform as a referee, I climb a knoll and pass the time with Major Othmar Huber, who hands me his card. Honeywell, Zurich. Like Strub, he grew up here. He once led artillery units, and is now in charge of infantry munitions. The fog has become so thick I cannot see thirty feet beyond him. We are alone on this knoll, like deserted sailors on an island. "We prepare for something well and hope it never happens," he is saying. "We think it necessary. When a Lebanon, a Falklands, an Afghanistan occurs, we analyze each. We try to transform the experience to our purposes."

The fluctuating fog is in recession again, and Strub and other officers are talking in a circle by the school. Close to them, a soldier lies prone on the ground. He has cut some branches from a bush and arranged them over his bazooka. The situation makes him smile. His name is Urs Märchy, and he is a salesman for Sulzer Brothers, Zurich. Two young boys walk by, glance at him without comment or apparent interest—a man with a bazooka lying on the ground outside their school. An old man with a walking stick pays even less attention. The machine gunners we talked with in the orchard are now officially dead. Red infantry surprised them from behind. Their lieutenant died with them. In Strub's unit, half the men are gone. The others are regrouping, blaming the fog. While the officers confer, I stand a little apart, rapidly writing notes. Between my nose and my notepad, there suddenly appears the muzzle of a Sturmgewehr. I look up into the unsmiling eyes of a soldier.

"Sigi! Sigi!"

Strub sees what is happening, comes over, and explains. Leo Fässler, foreman in a factory on the Greifensee, lowers the gun.

It is five hours after midnight, and in absolute darkness the Section de Renseignements sleeps—a deep agglomerate sleep, without a stir. The door opens at one end of the room. Light falls on the nearer bunks. A corporal with a bullhorn voice calls out, "Messieurs, bonjour!"

Reveille is not known by that name here. Here it is called la diane. Call it what you will, the response is complete silence.

Ten minutes later, the corporal tries again. In the continuing silence, Massy alone concedes that he is conscious. Staring upward into the black, he says, "Il fait beau."

Minutes later, the corporal reappears in the doorway and sternly orders everyone up. When the corporal is gone, Massy remarks, "He is thinking that he is a general."

No one else has complained, moaned, stretched, turned over, lifted his head, sat up—or, in fact, moved. When Lieutenant Wyssa arrives, he says exactly nothing, and they begin to stir. They dress, fill their packs. They breakfast on bread and fruit confections. They receive their assignments, calculate itineraries, and prepare for an arduous day. The enemy is everywhere—threatening passes, threatening the hanging valleys, threatening the riparian landscapes of the Rhone. A command post has been established in a small garage in a private home. In addition to the usual note-taking and sketchmaking and assessments of bridges and barns, the patrol today will carry a transceiver and report to the command post coded descriptions of activity in the Valais.

The sky is heavy, but there is brightness at the southern edge. With their packs and assault rifles, the patrol sets out. Walking downhill—among cattle and barns and apple trees in fruit—Jean-Bruno Wettstein tells me that during my absence the Section de Renseignements was visited by Divisionnaire Tschumy. "He said he believed that Switzerland must be defended from the borders by the army. He said a lot of young people, basing their views on Che Guevara and the French Maquis, think guerrilla warfare is the answer, but actually to depend from the outset on guerrilla warfare is to permit your cities to be occupied, and therefore to capitulate. He said, 'We don't want to be occupied. The army must be prepared to meet an invader head-on, because guerrilla warfare is particularly hard on civilians.' The Swiss remember Oradour, the French village that was almost totally murdered—and many similar examples. I believe Tschumy is right. Tschumy is realistic. The Maquis may have been somewhat effective, but their country was already occupied."

A light rain begins to fall. Taking shelter under the

tall concrete pillars of the elevated Simplon road, the soldiers put on rain gear, and turn on the transceiver to send their first coded message: "THE REDS ARE USING POISON GAS AT GRIMSELPASS."

The code consists of three-digit numbers, which represent phrases that are recorded in a top-secret book. An infantry battalion, for example, is a 200. A message might read, "200 206 195 495 202 322 999." One does not easily learn to compose such tight prose, and in the Section de Renseignements there is particular need for practice.

"ROUGE A PARACHUTÉ SUR GRIMSELPASS."

"We are Boy Scouts," Wettstein comments as the message goes out.

They are, at any rate, four today—Massy, Wettstein, Pillard, and Pierre Gabus, a Geneva lawyer. They are descending into Brig—Roman Brig, staging point for travellers preparing to cross the Simplon, a historically imbricate town. To walk to its center from the outside is to go from basketball courts and light industry into neighborhoods of the nineteenth and eighteenth centuries and on into Renaissance vestiges and cobblestoned medieval streets. In the covered Metzgergasse, the soldiers step out of the rain and transmit another message: "RED ARTILLERY IS HITTING THE NUFENENPASS."

They have leaned their rifles against the window of a textile shop, in front of a display of cotton sweatshirts, on one of which is lettered "U.S. BASEBALL NEW YORK."

"U.S. cultural infiltration," Wettstein remarks. "That is a typical Swiss shirt."

It is true. In all parts of Switzerland, people wear shirts that say "CALIFORNIA UNIVERSITY" or "FLORIDA UNIVERSITY" or "NEW YORK UNIVERSITY." One afternoon among the walking rich on the Bahnhofstrasse in Zurich, I saw a tall young woman roasting and selling chestnuts, her ocean-swell breasts filling a Harvard sweatshirt.

The rain stops. The patrol moves on, and passes a Bridge of Sighs connecting two parts of a seventeenth-century palace. Wettstein says, "Now forget the army for a minute and look at that."

In Sebastiansplatz, everyone stops to drink at the fountain commemorating George Chávez, the first man to fly out of Switzerland and cross the Alps in an airplane. He crashed and died on the other side.

On the Bahnhofstrasse of Brig are many shoppers, none of whom shows any surprise on seeing a patrol of soldiers with assault rifles coming down the street, just as the citizens of Oberarth were not surprised to find a battle taking place in their town. Massy's attention is arrested by a Prontophot booth in the foyer of a Jelmoli store opposite the Walliser Kantonalbank. For a coin or two, the booth will produce a passport-size photograph. The soldiers stack their rifles against a table of dry flowers, for sale in bunches, two francs a bunch. All five of us, stacked one on another, under Massy's direction assemble in the booth. We freeze before the lens. While we wait for the picture, a message goes out, Prontophot booth to command post, now hear this: "ONE COMPANY OF MOTORIZED ENEMY FUSILIERS HAS LANDED IN HELICOPTERS BETWEEN MÜNSTER AND THE RHONE. AN ENEMY SECTION DE RENSEIGNEMENTS HAS CROSSED THE NIEDERWALD." It appears that we have a red rival.

Having traversed the city, the patrol reaches the Rhone—here a green running river with frequent patches of white. There are two bridges not far apart. Massy sketches them and records data on their structures and dimensions. The soldiers cross the river, walk downstream along the right bank, and stop to admire a big steel bucket that slides several hundred metres down a cable, splashes into the rapids, picks up a few tons of gravel, and emerges from the river to ascend to a cement plant. After the big steel bucket has made six round trips, they turn and face the Bernese Oberland. It begins only a few feet away, as the terrain rises sharply from the river.

According to instructions, the patrol is to climb some distance and check out possibilities. The first possibility is that we will fall off the cliffside into the Rhone. The climb is efficient, in the sense that almost every step is up. Where the going is particularly steep, there are cables to hang on to—put here, says Massy, by farmers. It is a trail of short switchbacks, now among scattered trees, now across rock face. Astonishingly soon, the view expands. The Rhone seems a long plunge below. In Brig, over the river, we can see the green where the battalion held its Prise du Drapeau, the marble yard, the Saltina coming down from Simplon, the twin dark holes of the railway tunnels to Italy. In the long perspective to the west, the walls of the Rhone Valley seem to come together and close. In the middle ground is the jet strip at Turtmann. Massy is reciting numbers into the walkie-talkie: "A COMPANY OF SWISS FUSILIERS IS WITH DIFFICULTY HOLDING TURTMANN." The sun comes and goes in a sky of breaking cloud.

In all, we climb about fourteen hundred feet before the terrain leans back—as a pronouncedly inclined alpage. The view is now panoptic—over the deep-set river to the white summits, the long front line of the

Pennines leading the eye west. Twenty miles down-stream, the valley bends slightly and cuts the view. Above the river, avalanche tracks stripe the mountain-sides between dark gorges no machine could pass. The floor of the valley is groomed and industrial. There are rows of Lombardy poplars along airstrips that serve no city. This centerland of the Valais, with its vegetable fields and orchards, too—its apples and asparagus, to-matoes and pears—would appear to be an ultimate citadel for the democracy, where the nation could attempt an impregnable stand. As if the mountains were not barrier enough, ancient landslides have left their natural barri-cades at intervals down the valley.

A farmhouse near the alpage is checked out for water and habitation. There is enough of both for one company. We make our way on upward and—with some surprise, as always—climb onto a curving moun-tain road.

"A COMPANY OF FUSILIERS HAS PARACHUTED INTO THE NUFENENPASS."

We walk west about a kilometre, with the Pennine Alps to our left, the Rhone deep below, and come into a vertical village, stacked up facing the sun. There is a restaurant called Restaurant. Inside is a long table by a window looking at the mountains. In the restaurant's umbrella stand the patrol stands four assault rifles. Half-litre glasses of beer are soon on the table by the window. The prospect is giddy—a long fall down the mountain-side and deep into le trou. I remember Lieutenant Strub saying, "Basically, with age, you become sly in the army, and you know in which restaurant you will find the soldiers, and the slyness is a military advantage if an enemy comes."

The walkie-talkie is set up on the table, its antenna inclining toward the light. Massy strings numbers with a pencil on a pad. He reports to the command post, "A COMPANY OF MOTORIZED RED FUSILIERS HAS DESCENDED FROM THE NUFENENPASS AND HAS REACHED ULRICHEN."

From Birgisch, as this village is called, the patrol is to return with an aerial sketch of the valley environs of Brig. Pierre Gabus looks out the window and draws one, deftly.

Fondue arrives—authoritative with kirsch and bubbling with the Fendant of Valais. An alcohol flame spreads flat on the bottom of the pot, browning the edges of the cheese inside. There is a transition from beer to wine. Massy pours. Wettstein says, "The army needs marginal people. They know that in an emergency if there's a job to be done we'll do it. That's why they leave us alone. We agree to walk and to shoot, but for us it is difficult to submit to discipline."

Long forks are flying. The fondue is surpassingly good. Four new customers have taken seats at a nearby table. They see the situation and are obviously amused. They are men, dressed in wool shirts, and are stopping in from work—farmers probably, at any rate civilians, but, of course, they are also in the army. They laugh. They jeer. They exhibit a mixture of mockery and empathy. When Massy lifts the transceiver and reads off a set of numbers, they moo in unison, helping the command post to imagine a bucolic scene.

"Moooo."

"LA GARE DE BRIGUE A ÉTÉ DÉTRUITE PAR LES SABOTEURS."

"Moooo."

"A BATTALION OF ENEMY MOTORIZED FUSILIERS HAS

LANDED IN HELICOPTERS IN THE PLAIN OF THE RHONE BE-
TWEEN TURTMANN AND THE RIVER."

"Compris! Compris! Moooo."

Massy holds the transceiver even higher, turns it
upside down, and stirs the fondue with the antenna. He
wipes it off and calls in another message: "A PEASANT
IN OBERWALD HAS SEEN FOUR ARMORED CARS COMING OUT
OF ST. NIKLAUS AND HEADING FOR THE VALLEY."

As the alcohol burns on, the golden crust is ever
more delicious, scraped from the edge of the fondue.
Dessert is coupe Danemark—four and a half francs'
worth of whipped cream over ice cream under ductile
chocolate. There are five wee glasses of kirsch.

Wettstein waxes declarative, saying, "This is the
best day I have spent in the Swiss Army."

On winter marches in the time of the Borgias, it was
thought that Swiss soldiers, in their cold armor, might
lose too much body heat. Accordingly, they were given
orders never to drink water but to quench all thirst with
schnapps.

"TWO COMPANIES OF ENEMY MOTORIZED FUSILIERS
HAVE REACHED RARON. ABOUT FIFTEEN ARMORED VEHICLES
HAVE BEEN DESTROYED."

Massy signals for a check and knocks back the last
of the kirsch. Again he lifts the transceiver. There is
more to report before we go.

"AN ATOMIC BOMB OF PETITE SIZE HAS BEEN DROPPED
ON SIERRE. OUR BARRICADES AT VISP STILL HOLD. THE
BRIDGES OF GRENGIOLS ARE SECURE. WE ARE IN CONTACT
WITH THE ENEMY."